INTO THE FIRE

FIVE RULES FOR IGNITING A LEADERSHIP LEGACY

Dr. Brandon Beck

Unlocking Unlimited Potential Publishing
Sleepy Hollow, NY

Copyright © 2025 by Brandon Beck

All rights reserved.

No part of this publication may be reproduced, distributed, or transmitted in any form or by any means, including photocopying, recording, or other electronic or mechanical methods, without permission in writing from the publisher.

Published by Unlocking Unlimited Potential Publishing
Sleepy Hollow, NY

Cover Design: Carlos Sanchez

Into The Fire: Five Rules for Igniting a Leadership Legacy
ISBN: 979-8-218-64505-2

Praise For *Into The Fire*

More books have been written on leadership than any subject on earth. *Into The Fire* ranks right up there with the best of them. Dr. Brandon Beck —acclaimed speaker, teacher, and coach— has written a book rich with clarity and passion —an empowering, story-driven roadmap that lays out a proven route to become the leader you want to be.

—Wayne Coffey, New York Times bestselling author of more than 30 books, among them *Above The Line*, a leadership book co-written with Urban Meyer

Brandon Beck's *Into the Fire* is a profoundly personal, high-impact guide that challenges leaders to embrace their journey, own their story, and transform experiences into leadership fuel. With a powerful blend of storytelling and actionable insights, Beck provides a roadmap for growth, equipping leaders at any level with the mindset and strategies to lead with confidence, purpose, and impact. This book doesn't just discuss leadership; it ignites it!

— Dr. David Arencibia, Speaker & Author of *Foundations of an Elite Culture*
Texas Principal of the Year
National Principal of the Year Finalist

Dr. Brandon Beck ignites the fire within with his leadership lessons and guidance. Integrating personal reflections and experiences with professional observations and assessments, this deeply personal book offers practical leadership guidance. Spanning industry and age, Beck's latest contribution to the field of leadership is impactful and should be on your shelf!

— Michael Lubelfeld, Ed.D., Superintendent & Author of *The Unfinished Leader, The Unlearning Leader*

Dr. Brandon Beck's book *Into The Fire - 5 Rules for Igniting a Leadership Legacy* does exactly what Dr. Beck set out to do in writing it; inspire and equip leaders to embrace their stories, empower their teams, and find clarity in their purpose. As leaders, we all know that it is our job to create, empower, and support future leaders. Throughout his book, Dr.

Beck shares leadership stories and outlines various strategies for using our stories to not only build the fire within ourselves but to ignite a fire in others. Allow this to become part of YOUR journey towards igniting your fire in greater ways than ever before!

— Coach Kurt Hines, Teacher, Speaker, Head Football Coach Coronado High School, CA, Author of *Called to Empower*

A fire burns deep within the soul of Dr. Brandon Beck, and he has put ink to pages, giving us a roadmap on how to ignite our own fire that will leave a legacy long after we are gone because of that fire and the way it led us to lead others. I personally have benefitted from Brandon's selfless coaching and knowledge in stoking the fire within to build my leadership capacity. This book gives you specific, detailed steps in how to find your fire and let it burn in a leadership role to impact others.

This book is a must-read if you want to leave a legacy with your leadership and stay on fire in why you do what you do.

— Kip Shubert, Teacher, Speaker, Coach, Author of *Struggle to Strength*

I can confidently say that *Into the Fire: 5 Rules for Igniting a Leadership Legacy* by Dr. Brandon Beck is a must-read for anyone looking to lead with purpose and authenticity. What sets *Into the Fire* apart is the raw honesty and vulnerability with which Brandon shares his story. The moment he describes facing death and emerging with a renewed sense of purpose is one you won't forget. Brandon reminds us that leadership isn't about avoiding the fire—it's about stepping into it with courage and conviction.

This book isn't just about leadership—it's about legacy. Brandon makes it clear that leadership isn't reserved for a select few; it's a calling we all have the opportunity to answer. If you've ever doubted your ability to lead, *Into the Fire* will ignite that belief and give you the tools to make a lasting impact. Whether you're leading a team, a classroom, or simply trying to make a difference in your community, *Into the Fire* will challenge you to step up, embrace the heat, and lead with unwavering purpose.

— Tom Pesce, Speaker, Educator, Magician

INTO THE FIRE

Through powerful storytelling and authentic vulnerability, Dr. Brandon Beck masterfully demonstrates that true leadership begins when we own our stories. Into the Fire doesn't just inspire you to lead—it equips you with actionable principles for transforming pivotal moments into enduring strengths. Brandon beautifully captures how leadership isn't about authority, but about leaning into your team, cultivating leadership in others, and intentionally crafting a legacy that lasts. This book is essential for any leader ready to step fully into their purpose.

—Dr. Darrin Peppard, Speaker, Leadership Expert, Author of *Road to Awesome* and co-author *Culture First Classrooms*

Dedication

To my Girls…Stephanie, Lyla, Maeve, Gemma, and Peaches
Thank you for leading the way.

TABLE OF CONTENTS

Introduction 1

RULE 1: IDENTIFY THE FIRE WITHIN
Unshakeable Confidence is Paramount 10
Everyone Needs a Coach 11
Results Coaching 13
Set Up Goals for Success 14
Fostering A Culture of Goal-Setting 16

RULE 2: TURN YOUR STORY INTO POWER
Learning Disabled 22
The 3 Influences of Your Self-Confidence 25
    Story 26
    WHY 27
    Purpose 28
3 Questions to Turn Your Story Into Power 29
Write Your Purpose Statement 35
Professor J 37

RULE 3: LEADERS CREATE LEADERS
A Leader's Impact is Endless 42
Do You Believe You Are A Leader? 43
Leaders Create Leaders 44
The Transformational Leader 45
The Transactional Leader 46
Forged in the Fire 47
You Can't Bring a Dog With You to Class! 48
Flow With the Fire 50
#UUPotential Stories Show 52
The 3 E's of Transformational Leadership 54
Juan's Story 58

RULE 4: EVERY TEAMMATE MATTERS
Leading with Values 64
What is your mana? 65
Purposeful Mantras 66
2018 Mantra: "Trust the Process" 67
Pygmalion Effect 69
Celebrating the W.I.N.S. 71
Lead the Pack 74
When Leadership Speaks Louder Than Words 75

RULE 5: YOU BELONG AS A LEADER
Uncle John 81
Fueling a Legacy 84
The Entrepreneur Mindset 86
Become Unbeaten 87
The Two-Minute Culture Test 90
The 4 C's of Positive Team Culture 91
Igniting a Leadership Legacy 94

References 99
Acknowledgements 101
About The Author 103

Introduction

Leadership is more than a title—it's a responsibility, a mindset, and a commitment to lasting impact. *Into the Fire: Five Rules for Igniting a Leadership Legacy* is for those who are ready to step boldly into their role, embrace challenges, and leave a meaningful mark on the teams, groups, and organizations they lead.

Throughout this book, we discuss leadership's impact on groups of people, often using words like *team, group,* or *organization.* No matter what term resonates most with you, the rules in these pages are designed for leaders committed to strengthening self-confidence, shaping team culture, and building a lasting legacy.

This book is built on the belief that leadership starts from within. Through five foundational rules, you'll explore leadership stories, powerful lessons, and transformative insights that will help you grow, lead with purpose, and ignite lasting change:

Rule 1: Identify the Fire Within
Rule 2: Turn Your Story Into Power
Rule 3: Leaders Create Leaders
Rule 4: Every Teammate Matters
Rule 5: You Belong as a Leader

Each rule is grounded in real experiences, hard-won lessons, and the inspiring stories of those who have overcome challenges to find leadership success. Every chapter is designed to challenge you, inspire reflection, and provide actionable steps to elevate your leadership.

Whether you're a seasoned leader or just stepping into your role, this book will serve as a guide to unlocking your full potential and empowering those around you.

It's time to step *Into The Fire*—and lead with purpose.

RULE 1

IDENTIFY THE FIRE WITHIN

> *"There were a series of moments that led you here. We must explore their foundation."*

I had to light myself on fire to write this book for you.

I had to light myself on fire to realize that I was on the wrong path. And I had to light myself on fire in order to learn important lessons about self-confidence and leadership.

It was a fire that once tried to end my life, but a moment where I was given a second chance. And that second chance would become something that would lead me toward becoming an award-winning teacher, coach, speaker, and leadership coach.

In fact, your leadership journey didn't start today—it began in the moments that shaped you, the lessons that challenged you, and the fire that fuels your desire to grow.

INTO THE FIRE

To understand the significance of this fire, I need to take you back to a camping trip in upstate New York. When I was 14 years old, I went camping with a group of friends who I really wanted to impress. This particular group of kids would always go camping without parents, so when they finally invited me, I was determined to prove that I belonged.

When I arrived at my friend's house, we walked about 100 yards into the woods behind his house. We made it to the cabin that his father built, which overlooked a stream. I noticed there was an empty fire pit. Wanting to be useful, I ran into the woods to gather firewood. After several trips, I had collected a massive pile.

"Beck, you got a ton of wood! We are going to have a huge fire tonight!" one of my friends exclaimed.

I was feeling pretty proud at this point, but then another friend came out from behind the cabin carrying a bright red gasoline can that was normally used to fuel the tractor, and he shouted, "Yeah guys, we are going to have a REALLY BIG FIRE TONIGHT!"

Everyone started stacking the wood in the fire pit, piling it higher than our heads. We were about to have a massive bonfire. As we were getting ready to light the fire, one of my friends shouted, pointing to the gasoline can in his hand, "Guys…you're forgetting something…" He started dousing the wood.

Then, he lit the pack of matches on fire and threw it on the gasoline-soaked logs.

"POOF!"

The fire exploded into the sky with flames reaching over ten feet high. The heat forced us to push our chairs back. As the night wore on, anxiety crept in. I was afraid—afraid of sleeping in a cabin so far from my parents, afraid of the gasoline, and afraid that we were inching closer to a bad decision.

All of a sudden, out of the corner of my eye, I saw one of my friends splash another cup of gasoline on the fire.

IDENTIFY THE FIRE WITHIN

Everyone cheered! Everyone thought it was the coolest thing… everyone except me! I got really scared, and one of them saw the fear on my face and made fun of me…

"Beck, WHY are you so scared?"

Without even thinking, I jumped out of my chair, grabbed the gasoline container, filled the closest cup to the brim, looked straight into his eyes, and said, "I'll show you who is scared!"

And then…I heaved the giant cup of gasoline into the fire.
That's when the fire came running toward me like an angry animal, and I became engulfed in flames…

I WAS ON FIRE!

I fell to the ground and did the only thing I could think of…*Stop, Drop, and Roll.* It wasn't working! My friend took his shirt off and started hitting me, trying to smother the fire into submission…nothing was working. 40 seconds…45…50…now, at this point, I am really starting to think…there is nothing I can do…I am going to die here tonight, all because I was trying to impress these kids…all because I wanted to be accepted as someone who was unafraid.

As I was rolling back and forth…I slowly began to see the end coming…I was helpless…we had done everything we could have thought of at that moment…and nothing was working.

Then… all of a sudden…I heard a word flash across my brain…

"STREAM!"

The word ran through me like a giant freight train, and it lifted me to my feet. I immediately remembered there was a stream about 30 feet away in the darkness. I jumped up and sprinted until I fell face-first into the 12 inches of water.

"Ssssssssssss……" the sizzling sound of my skin as the smoke dissipated into the sky.

INTO THE FIRE

I was burnt horribly from the waist down. As I shined the flashlight on my legs, what I saw was horrifying. Long, yellowish, oozing blisters ran up and down my legs. Black, charred, and white skin poked through my shorts and socks. My shorts and socks hung in tatters with burnt edges.

We needed help. We had no choice but to tell my friend's mom what happened—how everything went horribly wrong in an instant. And it was all because of me. Everyone would get in trouble. Parents would warn their kids to stay away from me, calling me a bad influence.

I was hospitalized with deep second and third-degree burns. I couldn't walk for six weeks. Every day, visiting nurses came to my house to change my bandages.

As I sat home during the rest of the summer before I entered high school, I became depressed and confused about my purpose in life. I had tried to prove my worth to others by doing something I truly regretted.

However, I was still alive.

I would have scars for the rest of my life. Scars that were reminders of a dumb decision that I made to try and impress others because I didn't have enough confidence in myself.

After coming so close to losing my life, I learned something very important.

We all encounter moments where we feel the urge to prove ourselves to others, but true strength lies in understanding that our worth isn't defined by external approval—it's forged by the fire within us.

I stopped focusing on the fires that were happening around me. And I started focusing on the fire inside of me.

True leadership begins the moment we stop seeking approval from others and start fueling the fire within. The only validation that truly matters is the one we give ourselves.

I realized it was time for me to step into becoming a leader in my own life instead of letting others determine who I was going to be. I redirected my attention from the external chaos to the internal flame, igniting personal growth. This is the leadership flame that exists inside of us all. And I knew that flame inside of me was destined to inspire other leaders to make a greater impact.

Identify the Fire Within

True leadership begins when we stop chasing approval and start igniting the fire within. With that flame lies the potential to change lives, starting with your own. The only validation that truly matters is the one we give ourselves.

Understanding why your leadership fire is lit will allow you to keep it burning. In fact, there were a series of moments that led you to open up this book. Whether you are a teacher, student, athlete, coach, or CEO, you are a LEADER. We have crossed paths for a very important reason.

Your leadership journey didn't begin today—it started in the moments that shaped you, the challenges that tested you, and the fire that fueled your growth.

It is important we explore the foundation of your leadership fire because inside these moments are humongous opportunities for growth.

I hail from two teachers as parents. My mother taught middle school English for 35 years, and my father taught history in high school for 37 years.

My parents were very good teachers. Some of the best that I have ever seen in a school. Both were different in their style, but they were highly successful educators who were passionate about getting the absolute best out of their students. My mother was the creative, innovative, and storytelling teacher that all students loved. My father was the knowledgeable Advanced Placement teacher who prided himself in teaching History to teenagers in the upper echelon of high school academics.

In addition, both of them found unique ways to connect with students beyond the classroom setting. My mother was a drama teacher, taking her creativity and inspiration to the stage by producing numerous school performances. She encouraged me to face my fears and introduced me to speaking on stage, developing stage confidence. My father was a high school soccer coach and also developed the "International Club." This club took students on trips to New York City, Montreal, Boston, and beyond. They also worked closely with a program that would bring exchange students from other countries to different high schools in the area. They believed in the importance of culture and its strength in the development of human beings.

Needless to say, I was inspired by these two extremely passionate educators, first and foremost, to become an educator. I wanted to pick up where they left off. Even as a young child, I naturally noticed their passion and drive to develop others around them. At the dinner table, I would hear the good, the bad, and the ugly of their classroom interactions, but I was never steered off my path. I wanted to teach. I wanted to coach. There seemed no better environment for me than a school.

The fire that nearly burned me down instead ignited a more profound purpose within me—to serve others. It led me to a life of teaching and coaching, shaping my journey in ways I never expected. That same fire fuels my mission: to help leaders ignite their leadership legacy.

I participated in unique educational experiences as a snowboard instructor, soccer coach, and outdoor education teacher in high school and college. Those greatly influenced my ability to understand dynamic learning styles. Since the age of nine, I've been an entrepreneur, constantly seeking new opportunities to grow and inspire others.

I'm also a proud father of three girls and a devoted husband. In my journey to support student leadership, I adopted a dog named Peaches, who joined me at school to help students discover their own leadership potential. Each of these experiences has prepared me with the tools to develop deeper connections with those I am fortunate to lead.

Because of the fire, I earned National Board Certification, a Doctorate in Educational Leadership, and wrote *Unlocking Unlimited Potential*. These milestones sparked a deeper curiosity in me, driving me to learn through the stories of others on my podcast, *The Unlocking Unlimited Potential Stories Show*. Over the years, I have had the privilege of interviewing more than 125 thought leaders in education and business, exploring what makes them so confident as leaders and how they have cultivated confidence in their environment.

Now, let me be clear. Writing a book, a degree, a certificate, or even hosting a podcast does not make me the best educator or leader. I know that. But I want you to understand that this work is deeply rooted in extensive research, drawing from the insights of psychologists, sociologists, personal development experts, educational leaders, CEOs, professional athletes, motivational speakers, athletic coaches, real-life teachers, and more.

All of this was possible because the fire did not take my life that day. It taught me an invaluable lesson about the role of self-confidence in unlocking leadership potential. Whether coaching sports, teaching, being a student leader, or stepping into entrepreneurship, the common thread is: self-confidence. When we feel prepared, we believe in our ability to succeed, which fuels hope. And inside that hope lies tremendous power. This book will show you how to harness and use that power to your advantage.

The most uniquely positioned leaders are those who believe in the unlimited potential of others. I believe in the unlimited potential of all individuals, and I believe that your potential as a leader is unlimited. This potential is nurtured by developing an understanding of your ability to control your mindset. Your thoughts and beliefs are where your actions begin, and those actions must aim to positively impact others in your school, locker room, business, and community. Your brain holds a Colosseum of possibilities. It requires training to endure the battle of emotions as you seek to unleash the unlimited potential in those you lead.

The ultimate goal of all leaders is to unlock the unlimited potential of those they serve. To do that, you must first identify the leadership fire that burns within you.

What makes you confident enough to take your seat on the roller coaster of emotions that the leadership journey consists of?

When you run Into The Fire, you're pushing through the senseless noise and the self-limiting beliefs that hold you back. It's about harnessing the flame that burns inside you. Within that flame lies hidden potential—potential that, once understood, can lead to incredible results in your life.

Unshakeable Confidence is Paramount

Self-confidence is the foundation of your leadership potential, and your leadership potential is deeply tied to your story. The way you see yourself as a leader begins with the stories you tell yourself. If you do not feel prepared or confident enough to do something, it is crucial to understand why. Your self-confidence stems from the defining moments in your life. These are the stories that shape who you are as a leader.

These moments are filled with lessons and hope. Stories of triumph, breakthroughs, and embracing challenges are rich with inspiration and guidance. Looking back on them can provide the fuel you need to navigate your leadership journey.

Self-confidence also comes from a belief that your surrounding environment is controllable. Those with high levels of confidence visualize success, set optimistic goals, and maintain a positive outlook when creating solutions to challenges. On the other hand, a lack of confidence often stems from negative self-perceptions or "self-limiting beliefs," which undermine motivation and performance.

When you learn to cultivate self-confidence, you unlock your potential to inspire others and lead with purpose. It is no surprise that confident leaders naturally draw others to follow them. Confidence is contagious, and it has the power to ignite the limitless potential in everyone around you.

Sometimes, you do not begin a mission with the intention of being chosen as the leader. Leadership often finds you when you least expect it, calling on you to step up in an instant or during a crisis. While challenging, these moments offer some of the most profound leadership lessons. They teach resilience, decisiveness, and the importance of staying grounded in your values.

When we take the time to reflect on our leadership stories, we uncover the foundation of our unshakeable confidence. These stories reveal how we rose to challenges, how we adapted in the face of uncertainty, and how we inspired others to move forward despite obstacles. Each experience, whether big or small, contributes to the tapestry of who we are as leaders.

Everyone Needs a Coach

On the day of my college graduation, I stood in my cap and gown, ready to head out the door, when a phone call came that would change the trajectory of my future.

After graduation, I was planning to move back to New York, not to my familiar upstate roots, but to Westchester County, NY, a suburban area about 30 miles outside of New York City. This move marked a significant transition. I was leaving behind an opportunity to play semi-professional soccer to begin my career as an educator, stepping into a more densely populated community where I had few connections.

On the other end of the phone call was a local soccer coach from Westchester offering me the chance to coach varsity soccer at Briarcliff Manor High School. I accepted, not knowing then just how impactful this opportunity would become. One year later, after teaching in the Bronx, NY, for my first year, I landed a job at a school in the town next to the high school where I had been coaching. The sparks ignited just at the right moment.

This school would become my home as a teacher, and this soccer program would become my passion to lead for the next 19 years. Over these 19 seasons, our coaching staff led the program to an impressive record of 196 wins, 91 losses, and 21 ties. Together, we achieved seven league championships, two sectional championships, one New York State regional championship, and one State runner-up. I was also honored to be named League Coach of the Year six times and coach of the Section once.

Beyond the accolades, the most meaningful part of this journey has been the countless memorable experiences shared with high school athletes on and off the soccer field, shaping the program's legacy and my own in ways I could never have imagined.

In addition to being a High School soccer coach, I became a leader of a premier soccer organization that services over 2500 families in Westchester County, NY. We provide youth soccer programs for all levels of soccer, ages 3-23. We develop coaches, deliver curriculum, and implement coaching education to improve the quality of soccer in local towns in the New York metropolitan area. We also have a foundation that raises money to supplement the cost of premier soccer programs so all kids can participate in the experience regardless of their financial position.

Being a coach is a massive passion of mine, and I truly believe it makes me a more effective teacher and leader. However, when the COVID-19 pandemic hit, all of a sudden, there were no soccer fields to coach on. Our soccer club was put under massive stress as a business. For the first time, we had to navigate how to support our coaches and our entire staff while so many programs were canceled and outdoor training sessions were no longer possible.

Having co-managed the club with two business partners for a decade, we had never encountered a crisis of this magnitude. Families began calling and requesting refunds. We were determined to respond with honesty and fairness during such a difficult time. To ensure transparency and care, we decided to address every concern personally, through countless phone calls with anyone who had an issue, because we wanted our families to know we were being as proactive and compassionate as possible.

Before many schools established virtual programs, our soccer club had already adapted. We worked tirelessly to provide value to our players and their families. We launched online programs to keep our community connected and ensure we could still spend meaningful time together. This was a testament to our commitment to the sport and the people who make it so special.

The phone calls were going well, and we were able to address the concerns of everyone who had additional issues. However, the process nearly broke us. One of my business partners was in a serious bicycle accident that left him hospitalized. I immediately stepped in, taking on his share of the calls, determined to keep things running until he recovered. But the relentless effort pushed me to my limit as well. I ended up in the hospital with chest pains, convinced I was having a heart attack.

We were trying so hard to solve every problem and make every person happy, handling each concern one conversation at a time. Our business was surviving, but its leaders were not. Being away from the soccer fields was something I had never experienced before, and reaching my breaking point forced me to see things from a new perspective.

I had defended a dissertation several years earlier. I had always said, "I am going to write a book." So I decided to start writing. My first book, *Unlocking Unlimited Potential,* was published in 2020, and I began to get invited to speak to teachers and school leaders about this work. Then, athletic programs asked me to speak to their athletes and coaches. Soon, I was being asked to speak on various stages, reaching a wide range of audiences.

Suddenly, I began to see the profound impact my leadership story had on others. I was hearing their leadership stories, building meaningful connections, and experiencing immense joy in the process. As I shared my journey, I found purpose in helping others cultivate leadership confidence, knowing it would ultimately strengthen and enrich the positive culture of their entire organization.

I didn't seek out this path; the fire within me drew me to it.

That same fire exists within you. It has been shaped by your experiences, strengthened by your challenges, and fueled by your passion. You do not need to search for it—it has been burning inside you all along. True leadership begins when you embrace that fire, trust its power, and let it illuminate the path ahead.

When I dove into the stream that night and heard the sizzling sound of my skin as the fire went out, a new spark caught flame inside of my heart. It was the awakening of my fervor to write, speak, teach, and coach leaders. This was a revelation that had eluded me for nearly three decades.

As I reflect on these pivotal moments, I realize how they illuminated the path to my true calling. Each defining moment in our lives serves as a catalyst, igniting the flames of passion that shape our journey. These sparks, scattered across the landscape of our memories, form the very foundation upon which our deepest passions are built. They are the essence of our purpose, guiding us toward fulfillment and driving us to share our gifts with the world.

Results Coaching

Achieving your goals and dreams often takes a village. Identifying the fire within you—the passion that drives your leadership—requires guidance and discomfort. Your journey was never meant to be walked alone. A results coach helps push you beyond your comfort zone, challenging you in ways that spark growth. True transformation happens in those moments of discomfort, where the fire within you is tested and strengthened.

After writing *Unlocking Unlimited Potential*, I met Dr. Darrin Peppard, a fellow author and school leader who shared my passion for coaching people toward positive results. Darrin is a former school leader, speaker, publisher, and author of *Road to Awesome*. After reading his book, I reached out, and the rest is history. We both had an innate passion for leadership coaching. We quickly realized that many educators wanted to leverage their experience to publish a book, start speaking, develop a side business, and more. Recognizing this need, Darrin and I created a system to coach these leaders toward achieving their goals.

We were blown away by this program's impact on these thought leaders. As they began achieving success, their progress inspired us to keep going. We expanded our work beyond education, created an online course, and became deeply committed to helping ambitious individuals maximize their impact. The ripple effect was undeniable—people saw real results, inspired others, and ultimately unlocked even greater success.

So, what was the secret to our success?

The Inspire-Connect-Launch Action Plan!

Everyone has a long list of dreams and goals, but our system emphasizes the power of a singular focus on managing one goal at a time. Too often, distractions derail progress, preventing us from reaching our full potential. The key is to choose one goal, develop a clear plan, and execute the necessary action steps with intention. But in order to do this, you must deeply connect this goal to your Story-Why-Purpose. By focusing on one objective at a time, success becomes not just possible but inevitable.

Set Up Goals for Success

We utilize the *Inspire-Connect-Launch Action Plan* (Figure 1) when coaching our clients. This Action Plan can be used with both adults and adolescents.

It's a system that transforms vision into a specific, measurable goal and fuels a purpose-driven plan for success. We have seen significant success with individuals who have committed to this process.

One of the best examples of someone I've worked with who has used this system with remarkable efficiency is the inspirational Kip Shubert.

I first met Kip in 2020 when he came to Darrin and me for leadership coaching. He wanted to write a book and grow his speaking business. Right away, we connected over our shared passion for coaching soccer and teaching. But what truly inspired me to support Kip wasn't just our common ground—it was his story.

Kip's journey took him from being a homeless alcoholic who had lost everything to becoming a thriving educator inspiring students in schools across the country. Like some of the other people you will read about in this book, he was a survivor of rock bottom. But he was not just surviving. He was a man on a mission. That mission allowed me to walk alongside him as he worked, dreamed, and developed his book from start to finish.

Very few people survive rock bottom and live to tell their stories. Even fewer rise from it, grow, and dedicate their lives to sharing their lessons with today's students and educators. Kip Shubert's story is a powerful testimony that challenges you to reach deep within your soul and define who you truly want to be.

Kip utilized the Inspire-Connect-Launch Action Plan in every way. He showed up prepared, took full ownership of the process, and worked step by step toward becoming a published author. After using it to release *Struggle to Strength*, he became even more relentless in his coaching and speaking career. In just two seasons, he transformed a struggling high school soccer program into a state powerhouse. At the same time, his speaking career grew from unpaid opportunities to consistent bookings across the country, where he now shares his story with audiences nationwide.

The Inspire-Connect-Launch Action Plan is a simple, effective process.

- **INSPIRE**= Define the result that inspires you.
- **CONNECT**= Align your story and WHY with your mission.
- **LAUNCH** = Outline the actionable steps, including estimated timeframes, to ensure a strategic and achievable plan.

Utilizing the guiding questions in *Figure 1* makes the Inspire-Connect-Launch Action Plan even easier to follow. The example provided below comes from one of Kip's Action Plans.

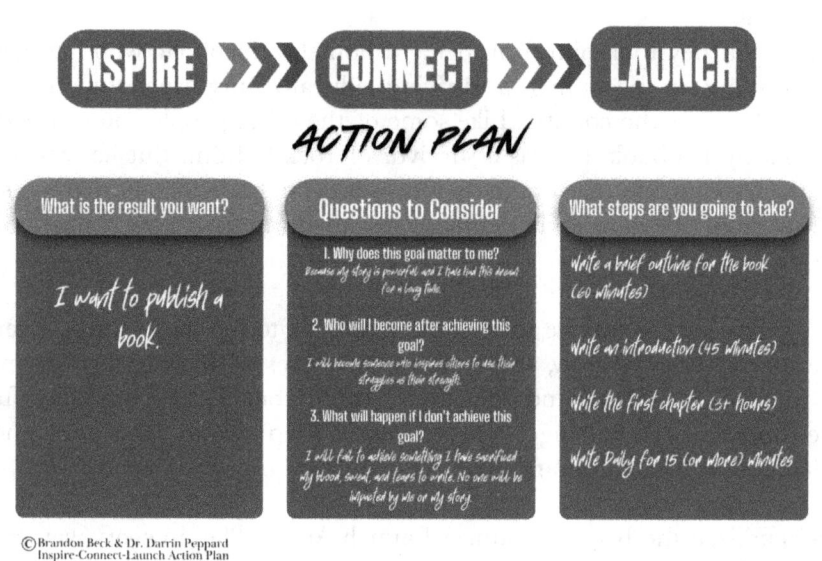

Figure 1: Inspire-Connect-Launch Action Plan

Fostering A Culture of Goal-Setting

Bob Proctor, once a high school dropout, became a renowned expert on the human mind, a best-selling author, and a global icon as a motivational speaker. He emphasized the power of the subconscious mind and the importance of goal setting, teaching that children are not empty vessels to be filled but are already brimming with potential.

Proctor believed that understanding the subconscious mind is essential to leadership development. He argued that goal setters and achievers are significantly more productive, often accomplishing more in a year than non-goal setters do in a lifetime.

The key to fostering a culture of goal-setting is leading by example. Proctor's advice to "walk your talk" means that leaders should actively write and track their own goals, demonstrating the value of the process. Committing time and effort to goal setting within a group enhances accountability, fosters healthy competition, and cultivates an environment where growth is valued.

Practice what you preach. This is an integral component of leadership that promotes a positive team culture. True leaders don't just talk about values; they embody them. And at the heart of it all is your leadership fire—the driving force that shapes your influence, energy, and impact.

Understanding the elements of your leadership fire is essential. What fuels you? What principles guide your actions? The more you refine and ignite this internal fire, the more powerful your leadership becomes.

Identify the Fire Within

The genesis of this work can be traced back to a pivotal moment in my life: surviving a harrowing fire at the formative age of 14. From that critical experience emerged a profound realization that it is the fire within us that propels us forward. This transformative event not only ignited my passion but also inspired an unwavering determination to lead and inspire others. Having come so close to the edge of existence, I discovered a newfound confidence in myself as a leader. I identified the fire within me, which became deeply rooted in my dedication to teaching and coaching. Since that day, I have been driven by an unyielding desire to ignite the flames of self-confidence and leadership in others.

This journey has been a relentless pursuit of knowledge and a quest to cultivate leadership confidence in those around me. I am profoundly grateful for the opportunity to traverse this path.

Just as a fire relies on heat, oxygen, and fuel to thrive, our self-confidence also depends on three essential elements: our story, our why, and our purpose. Each element is interconnected, creating a dynamic balance that fuels our growth as leaders.

Oxygen, symbolizing motivation, sustains the spark of our ambition. It is drawn from the stories we tell ourselves, the narratives that define who we are and who we aspire to become. These stories are often defining moments, rich with lessons from our past and visions for our future, and breathe life into our confidence. They help us navigate challenges, illuminate the possibilities ahead, and remind us of the resilience within.

Heat represents our WHY, the inner drive that is the foundation of our resolve. This heat is a source of energy and enthusiasm that grows stronger when we connect deeply with our purpose. It provides the enduring warmth we need to overcome setbacks, face adversity, and persist through life's storms. Once kindled, this internal fire transforms into an indomitable force, radiating strength and inspiring others along the way.

Fuel, derived from our purpose, is the sustaining element that keeps the flame alive. It is through purposeful action, aligning what we do with what truly matters to us, that our confidence grows. This alignment of intention and action provides the steady energy that drives our passion, allowing our efforts to gain momentum and meaning.

Together, these three elements—story, why, and purpose—work in harmony, mirroring the delicate yet powerful synergy of fire. When balanced and nurtured, they ignite a leadership flame within us, a fire that illuminates our path and serves as a beacon for leading others.

Our journey toward unshakeable leadership confidence is an ongoing process of embracing our story, connecting with our WHY, and acting with purpose. By tending to these elements, we can foster a steady and resilient inner fire that lights the way to personal growth, meaningful leadership, and an endless impact.

Before delving deeper into this book, a pivotal decision awaits you. You must embrace the realization that within your personal journey lie myriad stories, each marking significant defining moments of growth and self-discovery. As you embark on the next Rule: *Turn Your Story Into Power*, you'll need to discern which moments resonate most deeply with you, shaping your path forward. Embedded within these stories lies boundless potential waiting to be unearthed. It is through recognizing and embracing this potential that true transformation within your leadership journey becomes possible.

RULE 2

TURN YOUR STORY INTO POWER

"Your story matters. It tells us who you are and who you want to be."

-Unlocking Unlimited Potential Stories Show

For a kid who felt lost in the classroom, the soccer field became the one place where I discovered control, confidence, and the power to lead at a young age. It helped me turn my story into power.

School was a place where I constantly felt confused. I struggled to keep up in academics and watched in awe as others seemed to effortlessly absorb content. For me, sitting and listening to a teacher was like trying to catch water with my hands; it always slipped through. The confusion and frustration followed me daily, but my saving grace was the soccer field. As a goalkeeper, I discovered something extraordinary: the power of leadership. Like a quarterback in football, my position demanded focus, communication, and the ability to guide my team. In that position, I would eventually find clarity as a leader at a young age.

In elementary school, I was placed in remedial reading support, pulled out of the classroom, and left feeling defeated every single time I opened a book or saw another poor grade. Those grades told a story that planted seeds of self-doubt, strained my ability to make friends, and left me feeling powerless.

The struggles I faced in school became too big to overlook. Something was absolutely wrong, and it was clear that things needed to change.

Learning Disabled

Since both of my parents were teachers, they set upon a mission to figure this out. They extended themselves, leaving no stone unturned. They brought me to numerous doctors and I was succumbed to endless testing. After several months, I was labeled "Learning Disabled" and diagnosed with ADHD (Attention Deficit Hyperactivity Disorder). This diagnosis would extend even further into language processing delays that made learning and retaining information difficult. This label would end up following me through my entire academic career.

I was very fortunate that my parents knew the school system. They knew about Individualized Education Plans (IEPs) and became relentless in finding resources available in our school. I ended up with a laundry list of accommodations, from extra time on assessments to foreign language exemption and what felt like a life sentence to the "Resource Room."

I continued to struggle. I didn't understand how I learned best, and I relied on a ton of support from others to accomplish what other students were doing independently. I excelled in athletics, but in school, I struggled to learn. I would hide from my diagnosis as much as I possibly could. And as you learned previously from the fire story, I often felt the need to prove my worth to others. I acted out, misbehaved, got into trouble, and made some really poor decisions that led to even more trouble.

Yet, amidst the struggles, those seeds of self-doubt grew into something greater. By the time I had to choose a major in college, I knew exactly where I wanted to focus my energy: education. That decision was not born from chance but from a deeply personal conviction. My own journey, marked by challenges, mistakes, and the transformative impact of those who guided me, sparked a calling. I wanted to be for others what someone had been for me: a guide, a mentor, and a source of encouragement. This desire to turn my struggles into purpose fueled my determination to plant my roots in education and leadership.

At the age of eleven, I was confronted with a diagnosis that would shape my entire journey - a learning disability. This revelation marked a Defining Moment in my life, altering its course indefinitely. Surprisingly, this diagnosis became my source of resilience, guiding me through challenges and shaping my character. Looking back, it's clear that this diagnosis was not just a setback but a catalyst for self-discovery and the foundation upon which my leadership confidence was built. I learned to use this part of my story for power.

And I am going to teach you to turn your story into power in the pages that follow.

Figure 2: The Self-Confidence Cycle

The 3 Influences of Your Self-Confidence

When you open your eyes in the morning, your confidence begins its journey for the day. What is the story you are telling yourself about the day ahead? Are you anticipating success, or are you bracing for challenges? The narrative you create in those early moments sets the tone for how you approach every task, interaction, and decision. To harness the power of your story, you must first understand how your self-confidence fluctuates throughout the day. Confidence is not a constant; it ebbs and flows based on the tasks you engage in, the energy you bring, and the experiences you encounter. Some moments may feel effortless, while others test your resilience.

It is natural to feel completely assured in one area of your life while questioning your abilities in another. For instance, you might feel strong in one sport or a specific academic subject but second guess yourself when tackling a new skill or unfamiliar problem. These shifts are normal and rooted in your perception of competence and control in each situation. The key is to recognize these fluctuations, understand their sources, and intentionally recalibrate. When you embrace the ups and downs of confidence as part of your growth, you transform your internal dialogue into a powerful tool that fuels your potential.

For years, I have been obsessively researching, learning, speaking, and teaching about self-confidence, a topic that has fascinated me since my early days in education. Watching how people's mindsets impact their performance, their ability to lead, and their resilience has always intrigued me. Confidence is not just about skills; it is about the belief that you can navigate the unknown, handle setbacks, and show up fully, regardless of the circumstances. When you shift your mindset and learn to cultivate confidence intentionally, you discover the incredible capacity to reshape your narrative and, ultimately, your outcomes.

Self-confidence is the foundation of any desired result.

Your self-confidence is influenced by three things: Your Story, Your WHY, and Your Purpose. *Figure 2* describes the foundation on which your self-confidence is built. Your story, your WHY, and your purpose are the foundation of your self-confidence. Self-confidence is the root of all potential. When we feel deeply connected, prepared, excited, and passionate about achieving a result, we become more likely to execute a plan of action that leads to success.

Exploring your story will quickly connect you with the reason WHY you chose the path that you are on right now. Once your story and your WHY are connected, they will lead you toward a clear and concise purpose. Clarity in purpose ignites the flame of passion. Having clarity in your purpose will lead you to set goals, achieve dreams, and develop a more positive vision for your life.
Let's break it down further.

Your Story

Your story encompasses the narrative of your life, including your experiences, achievements, setbacks, and personal growth. These are your defining moments. These defining moments shape how you see yourself and influence your confidence. When you understand, embrace, and share your story, you uncover the power within your story. This exhibits your strengths, resilience, and capacity for growth, all of which build self-confidence.

Encourage others to share their own stories by creating opportunities for storytelling. This practice is vital for nurturing the flame that is in the power behind your story.

You cannot jump to conclusions about the behavior of someone you lead if you have not taken the time to learn their story. There is always a reason behind the way people treat or mistreat others. Sharing and learning the stories of others foster deeper connections and helps to dispel misunderstandings. Therefore, understanding others' stories enables you to lead more effectively.

As a teacher, I have had the privilege of working with students from diverse backgrounds and experiences. I have heard stories of children carrying their baby siblings across the border in the middle of the night, kids who have never experienced a vacation in their entire lives, and stories of divorce, loss, and unimaginable struggles.

I may never fully comprehend these stories, but listening to them is a profound way to understand why people behave the way they do.
Your story is one of the most powerful parts of who you are. In the previous chapter, we discussed identifying the fire within. That fire is

deeply connected to your defining moments and the reasons behind your journey. By reflecting on and embracing these moments, you gain clarity about your purpose and the unique path you are meant to follow.

All of us have such unique stories that come from our past experiences. Some of these experiences happened by natural selection, fate, process of elimination, or even accidentally (by luck). Regardless of the plot of your own story, you most certainly have one. It plays a massive role in your development as a leader. It is a significant part of WHY you feel the way you do about your career. Your story is full of many chapters with exciting twists and turns. However, it is your story. No one else's. It is so valuable to analyze your experiences to understand why you are where you are right now.

Your WHY

Your WHY is your motivation, the driving force behind every action you take, every thought you entertain, and every decision you make. It shapes the language of your life, framing how you see the world and how you interact with it. Your WHY is rooted in the defining moments that make up your story and reflects the core values that guide your behavior, aspirations, and sense of purpose. Clarifying your motivations allows you to connect deeply with your inner drive and passion, reinforcing your belief in yourself and your unique abilities. When your WHY aligns with your goals and values, it becomes a powerful source of self-confidence. It fuels your efforts, strengthens your resilience, and provides clarity during challenges.

The language you use consistently, both in your internal thoughts and how you communicate with others, is closely connected to your story and your WHY. Your words reflect your beliefs, shaping your mindset and influencing how you approach obstacles and opportunities. Positive and purposeful language reinforces your commitment to your goals, while language rooted in self-doubt or negativity can hinder your progress. When your words align with the essence of your WHY, you create a feedback loop of encouragement and motivation. This empowers you to pursue your aspirations with clarity and conviction. In this way, your WHY is not just a concept but a living and breathing force that actively shapes your journey.

Our lives are filled with stories that hold deep value and meaning, but it is up to us to choose whether we honor the voice of positivity or allow negativity to take control. This choice is one we make every moment of every day, shaping the narrative we live by. When we take the time to define WHY our fire is lit, we gain the ability to keep it burning. Understanding your WHY requires pushing past self-doubt and breaking free from limiting beliefs. It means staying connected to your story.

Your story fuels your sense of purpose and keeps your inner flame burning brightly.

Your Purpose

Your purpose is the overarching meaning and direction of your life. It represents the reason you exist and the actions you aspire to take. Understanding your purpose brings clarity and alignment with your values, serving as a compass to guide your choices and actions. It instills a deep sense of significance and fulfillment, nurturing your self-confidence as you pursue meaningful goals and strive to impact the world positively. The more precise your purpose becomes, the more focused and realistic you can be about achieving the results you are most passionate about.

Being purpose-driven means that your habits, goals, and commitments are intentionally aligned with your values and aspirations. It requires consistency, discipline, and a dedication to actions that reflect your character. These habits form the foundation of your daily life, allowing you to stay on track even in the face of challenges. Being purpose-driven ensures that your goals are not just ambitions but intentional steps toward a life of significance.

Your story, your WHY, and your purpose work together to shape your self-confidence. This connection empowers you to view challenges as opportunities for growth and to continue unlocking your unlimited potential as a leader of those you serve.

Now, let's take a closer look at these influences by examining three questions related to each element. As you explore these questions, I invite you to Reflect, Learn, and Grow—whether by pausing to jot down your thoughts or revisiting this section later.

3 Questions to Turn Your Story Into Power

There is a profound reason you have answered the call to lead. Your journey is not random; it is shaped by defining moments that have tested, refined, and revealed the essence of who you are. The lessons you have gathered from these pivotal experiences are not just memories. They are the foundation of your power and purpose as a leader. Take the time to identify the moments that resonate most deeply, and then look beyond the surface. Reflect on how these moments interconnect, weaving together a story that reveals not only where you have been but also why you are here, ready to lead today. Embrace the truth that your story holds transformative power not just for you but for those you are called to inspire.

Through my work, I have discovered that many leadership stories trace their roots to early academic or athletic experiences. These formative environments often serve as a common starting point in leadership journeys. They naturally present leadership opportunities through intentional selection, random chance, or even being "voluntold" to answer the call. Regardless of how it begins, these moments are pivotal because they reflect the faith someone once placed in you. After all, every leader has been inspired by another.

There is a deeper meaning behind these defining moments, school experiences, and the role models placed in your path to guide you toward leadership.

To understand why you are where you are today as a leader of others, you must consider three specific questions further *(Figure 3)*. Each question is related to one of the three influences of self-confidence and will guide you to connect your Story, your WHY, and your Purpose.

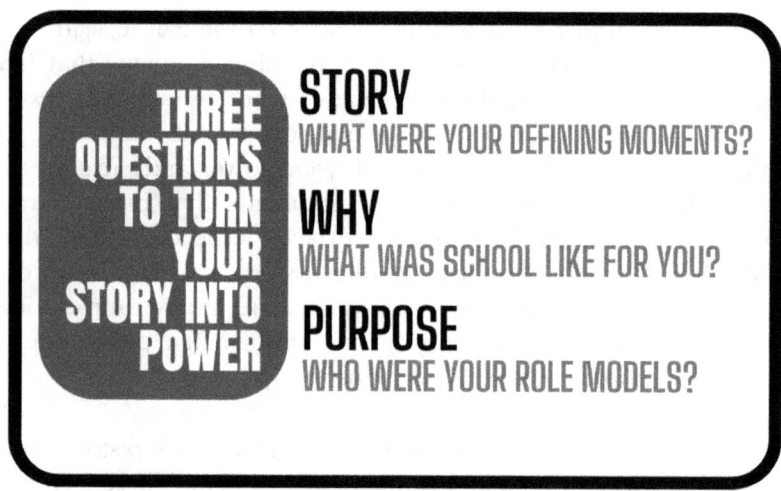

Figure 3: Three Questions to Turn Your Story Into Power

Story: What were your defining moments?

Now that you've listened to my stories, it's time to pause and reflect deeply within yourself. Reflect on the moments when you first felt the calling to become a leader. You may have fallen backward into it. Or you may have sensed this passion since childhood. And some might still be unraveling how they arrived here. Regardless, I assure you, there are invaluable moments within you that, once brought to the surface, will bring immediate reflection and wisdom. Your journey to this point has been marked by a series of significant moments worth exploring.

Being diagnosed as "Learning Disabled" and surviving that fire were two defining moments in my story that shaped the course of my life. In the aftermath of the fire, I felt a deep passion to teach others, driven by the desire to prevent them from repeating my mistakes. I was determined to help people understand that their value should never be dictated solely by others.

My journey continually brought me to spaces where I could support those struggling with self-limiting beliefs. Through these experiences, I gained profound insights into the power of self-confidence. This realization ignited a mission that repeatedly placed me in leadership roles, whether guiding a team, mentoring students, coaching educators, or inspiring other leaders.

After the fire, I began coaching soccer with an incredible mentor at the age of 15. It came naturally to me, and I was immediately drawn to seeing kids achieve. I will never forget when I first started coaching. I had so much joy giving back to others and instilling a love for the game, which helped me so much throughout my life. The opportunity to become a coach and a teacher quickly became a vision of mine that later became a reality.

I've come to believe that my survival was no accident; it was a calling. I am here to make the world a better place by empowering leaders to unlock their potential and leave a lasting impact.

When reflecting on your defining moments, remember that these experiences shaped the foundation of who you are today. Within each moment, there were decisions made, lessons learned, and events that left a lasting impact. Take time to revisit these pivotal experiences and create a list of them.

Then, for each defining moment, do the following:

> **REFLECT: Describe the moment:** Briefly describe the key event or experience.
> **LEARN: Highlight key details:** Note the significant decisions, lessons, or turning points within that moment.
> **GROW: Connect it to your leadership journey:** Reflect on how this moment has influenced the leader you've become today.

This exercise will help you uncover the powerful connections between your story and your leadership journey, allowing you to lead with greater authenticity and purpose.

WHY: What was school like for you?

Your journey as a student is a vital chapter in your story. Every school experience contributes a spark that shapes and ignites the fire behind the reason you lead the way you do. Each challenge, triumph, and connection plays a role in shaping the leader you are destined to become.

Maybe you had a terrible educational experience, struggled during specific grades or courses, or you just imagined your educational experience could have been so much different if your teacher understood who you were. You could have been bullied, struggled with friendships, or had a difficult upbringing. Or, you had such a positive experience in your schooling and may have even been chosen to be a leader at some point. We all experienced both educational stories. No matter your experiences, your journey through school was filled with endless leadership lessons.

One of the ultimate examples of a school experience shaping a leader is Daniel LaRusso from *The Karate Kid*.

Daniel LaRusso's experience at his new high school in *The Karate Kid* was a crucible that forged him into a stronger leader and champion. At just 14, Daniel was thrust into a world of adversity after moving from New York to Southern California, facing relentless bullying and physical abuse from a group of boys from the Cobra Kai Karate Dojo. Isolated and overwhelmed, Daniel's initial struggles were not just about survival; they were about finding belonging and purpose in an environment that seemed determined to break him. His school experience became the backdrop for his transformation, teaching him resilience and the importance of seeking growth over revenge.

Enter Mr. Miyagi, the wise mentor who protected Daniel and guided him on an emotional journey of self-discovery and development. Through unconventional methods such as the iconic "wax on, wax off" chores, Daniel learned perseverance, grit, and the power of self-confidence. These lessons were not just about mastering karate; they were about building the foundational traits of leadership. Daniel learned to turn his story into power. He channeled his frustrations into focus, his fear into courage, and his desire for revenge into a passion for personal growth.

At the end of the movie, which, at this point, I am crying uncontrollably and pumping my fists repeatedly toward the sky, everyone storms the mat to lift Daniel off the floor in celebration. Daniel's triumph was not merely about defeating Cobra Kai in a tournament; it was about rising above adversity with integrity and character. Throughout his difficult journey, Daniel learned that true leadership is about more than just winning—it's about handling challenges with courage, dignity, and self-respect. Through his school experience, Daniel gained the strength to lead with empathy and resilience, demonstrating that leadership is built on your school stories of overcoming obstacles, trusting oneself, and helping others rise to their potential.

Negative School Experience

REFLECT: Recall a difficult situation in school (challenging class, peer pressure, personal struggle).
LEARN: What happened? How did you respond?
GROW: What did you learn that shaped you as a leader?

Positive School Experience

REFLECT: Recall a moment of pride or success (excelling in a project, receiving recognition, helping others).
LEARN: How did it make you feel? Why?
GROW: What did you learn that shaped you as a leader?

Purpose: Who were your positive (and negative) role models?

Think about THAT leader, THAT teacher, or THAT coach for a moment. The one who inspired you most. The one who made you believe you could climb to the top of Mount Everest in a day. The one who made you feel love when no one else could. The one you were excited to be around. Who were the role models who showed you the way and inspired your leadership journey?

Everyone remembers their best teachers, leaders, or coaches, but let us not forget that we also remember our worst ones. Our experiences with other leaders are inspirational chapters to our story. Positive role models guide us toward who we achieve to be. Negative role models teach us what not to do, how not to treat someone, and how not to lead. The positive and negative role models that you had are incredibly impactful on your purpose as a leader.

You see, for me, being the product of two teachers, I was immediately drawn to the power of making a positive impact in the lives of others inside a school. Fast forward to my first year of teaching in the Bronx, NY. As a teacher commuting from the suburbs who attended high school in a rural town with very little cultural diversity, my first teaching job was definitely outside of my comfort zone. I started the year as a 4th-grade teacher, full of hope and determination to make a difference.

INTO THE FIRE

One month into the school year, I learned about New York City budgeting and what it means to be "excessed." Essentially, NYC schools report their enrollment after the first few weeks of the year, and the NYCDOE determines adjustments to balance the student-to-teacher ratio. In our case, this meant one teacher would be "excessed" and lose their job in October.

Sadly, someone lost their job that day—but it wasn't me. I was second to last on the list.

Instead, I lost the first class I ever had as a teacher. I had to walk into school and tell my 4th-grade students that, although we had a great start to the year, I would no longer be their teacher after that day. They were being reassigned to other 4th-grade classes, and I was taking over the 3rd-grade class of the teacher who had been let go.

I was less than a month into my first year of teaching. This truly tested my purpose as an educator. I had students who had already started to see progress and trust me. Tears streamed down their faces as they clung to me, pleading, "Why are you leaving us?" Their words cut deep, as though I was giving up on them. It was devastating and almost broke me.

My saving grace was Rachel Donnelly. As my first principal, she became the anchor I desperately needed. She had an incredible ability to lead with passion and confidence in an environment that often felt overwhelming and limited in resources. The teachers loved her, and I never doubted her belief in me.

Every day, Rachel lifted me up and supported me through the transition. When I felt like I didn't belong, she reminded me of my potential. Her empathy, unwavering support, and ability to inspire became a beacon of hope. She was the leadership role model I needed most during that time.

Looking back, I realize this moment didn't just test my purpose as an educator; it strengthened it. It taught me the value of resilience, the importance of connection, and the profound impact of a leader who believes in you when you need it most. Rachel's belief in me kept me in education and shaped the kind of leader I aspire to be for others.

When you think about your role models, it is important to consider the ones who always come to the forefront of your mind. These are the leaders who ignited a passion within you and inspired you to believe in your leadership potential.

To dig deeper into your role models, try this…

> **REFLECT:** Make a T-chart. On one side + and the other side −. List the names of a few positive and negative role models.
> **LEARN:** Next to each name, write the top 3-5 leadership qualities exhibited by that individual. *Examples: Trust, Listening, Integrity, impatient, selfish, etc.*
> **GROW:** Recognize the leadership qualities you value most from these role models and try incorporating them into your purpose statement.

To summarize, uncovering your leadership purpose begins by connecting your story, your WHY, and the experiences that have shaped you. Defining moments provide the foundation for understanding how your experiences have influenced your approach to leadership. Your school experiences, both positive and negative, further illuminate the reasons behind your passion and mission. Lastly, the role models in your life, whether they serve as shining examples or cautionary tales, help you identify the leadership qualities you value most.

By exploring these three questions, you can connect the threads of your journey and unearth a purpose that is uniquely yours. This clarity strengthens your ability to lead and equips you with the tools to inspire others.

Now, let us channel this insight into creating a powerful purpose statement, a statement that will serve as your guiding light in leadership and beyond.

Write Your Purpose Statement

A Purpose Statement is a cornerstone for any leader's journey. Writing one allows you to recalibrate and ensure your compass remains pointed toward your true north. In my workshops, I emphasize the value of crafting a Purpose Statement by asking participants to complete the following sentence at the beginning of our session:

"My purpose is to _____."

At the conclusion of the workshop, I ask them to revisit and complete the same sentence again. Without fail, attendees are amazed at how much deeper and more precise their purpose becomes after engaging in meaningful conversations and sharing personal stories.

It's a simple exercise, but the impact is profound. A clearly articulated Purpose Statement not only inspires but it also becomes a guiding force for authentic leadership.

Figure 4: Purpose Statement

After leading this workshop for my first 1,000 participants, I gathered feedback on their key takeaways. I compiled their responses into a word cloud, shown in *Figure 4*. This visual captures the recurring words and themes from leaders' purpose statements, providing a powerful snapshot of their collective insights.

To complete the Purpose Statement, do the following…

> **REFLECT:** Select one or two words that resonate deeply with who you are as a leader and fill in the blank. (Choose from the heart if you would like.)
> **LEARN:** Think about what you value most in your role as a leader—how you connect with, support, and inspire others.
> **GROW:** Put this statement somewhere you can see it often.

My purpose statement is: *"My purpose is to inspire and guide people to have faith in themselves and believe in their unlimited leadership potential."*

Your purpose statement embodies your Story and your WHY. Once you have dug into the depth of your personal story and developed a purpose statement, it needs to be placed somewhere you can see it daily. And if you are a true leader, you aim to be a role model and "lead by example." It serves as a temperature gauge for your success as a leader, allowing you to assess your level of commitment to your purpose statement each day.

Make sure you introduce your purpose to others so they know exactly how it represents you. Describe how it resembles your life's story, your goals, your visions, and your drive to be a better leader, student, and person. Describe what each word means. Take the time to answer any questions.

You can place it in your office, school, locker room, or home. You could even touch it every day like a Notre Dame Football player touches the "Play Like a Champion" sign as they walk out of the locker room onto the stadium field for a big game.

When you reflect on why you became a leader, it's inspiring to recognize that many of our earliest leaders were our teachers. These educators, our first role models, left an indelible mark with their stories and actions, fueling the fire of our purpose. I can still vividly recall one such teacher who helped me uncover my own purpose as a leader in our schools.

Professor J

One teacher who profoundly impacted my journey into education was Raymond Jobin, also known as "Professor J." His influence came at a pivotal time in my life.

After my first semester of college, my parents delivered devastating news—they were getting divorced. The announcement hit me hard, leaving me reeling with shock and pain. Their separation sent me into a downward spiral. My focus shattered, my grades fell, I failed critical exams and courses, and I began questioning whether I was meant to pursue a career in teaching. I felt adrift, uncertain about my future, and confused.

Amid this turmoil, I found myself in Professor J's class. He was a professor of one of the integral courses I would need to receive my teaching degree. One day, I fell asleep during a lecture. When he woke me, I sarcastically asked when class would end and, unhappy with his answer, blurted, "That sucks!" Instead of reacting angrily, Professor J calmly asked to speak with me after class.

After class, he revealed that other professors doubted my potential as a teacher. I had previously failed the state examination twice to get into the education program, and I was on my last chance. But he believed in me. He told me I had the ability to be a great teacher and promised to hold me accountable to that standard. His words were a wake-up call, a painful but necessary reminder that I was on the brink of giving up, but he was not giving up on me.

Professor J did not just see my struggles; he saw my potential. He embraced my unique way of thinking and encouraged me to channel it into becoming the best teacher I could be. His patience, honesty, and unwavering belief reignited a spark in me during a dark period of my life.

Seventeen years later, I was honored with the Teacher of the Year Award from my alma mater, and I was blown away when Professor J walked across the stage to present it to me. He recounted the story of our turning point with emotion, even mentioning a thank-you letter I had written him on the last day of class, a letter he still has framed on his desk at home. It was a letter in which I thanked him for helping me turn my story into power.

Without Professor J and that defining moment, this book would not exist. His faith in me changed the trajectory of my life and shaped the educator and person I am today.

Turn Your Story Into Power

As educators and leaders, we can never predict the power of our impact. And that impact will take you farther than any self-limiting belief ever will. There have been many defining moments that have led you along this path that you are on today. You have had times when you made difficult decisions, life-altering shifts, lost loved ones, and more, but you still keep finding ways to lead through it all. That energy inside of you is something special.

I began this chapter talking about being "Learning Disabled," a label that scarred me for my entire educational journey. Similarly, the fire that physically scarred me became a constant reminder of how close I had come to the edge of existence. These defining moments, though painful, were deeply connected to the path I ultimately chose for my career.

Through the guidance of incredible role models like Professor J, Principal Donnelly, and even the wisdom of fictional mentors like Mr. Miyagi, I began to uncover my WHY. At the time these events unfolded, I didn't realize their significance or the lessons they held. Yet, reflecting on those moments later allowed me to see their deeper meaning. Reconnecting with them brought clarity and fueled growth, helping me understand my purpose more profoundly.

Every single leadership fire requires heat, oxygen, and fuel to keep going. Inside each of those defining moments is a story worth exploring. This is the oxygen that breathes life into your purpose.

After all of these challenges, what is it that keeps you coming back for more? The answer: Your WHY. This is the heat of your fire, which represents your enthusiasm for the profession. The more deeply connected you are to your WHY, the closer you are to the love of your service.

Finally, your purpose fuels the fire within you. Clarity in your purpose allows you to set realistic goals, achieve more consistent results, and become more efficient. These influences on your self-confidence are present multiple times throughout every single experience in your life. Harnessing your story, staying connected to your WHY, and gaining clarity in your purpose will empower you to become a more impactful and effective leader.

As we've discussed the importance of purpose, it's crucial to recognize that true leadership goes beyond personal growth—it's about empowering others to lead as well. With that in mind, let's explore the next rule: *Leaders Create Leaders.*

RULE 3

Leaders Create Leaders

"The single biggest way to impact an organization is to focus on leadership development. There is almost no limit to the potential of an organization that recruits good people, raises them up as leaders, and continually develops them."

-John Maxwell

During my junior year of high school, I had the privilege of participating in a team-building program with my soccer team at a unique facility called the Adirondack Center, run by Craig Johnson, a former football coach from Villanova University. That visit, at age 16, profoundly impacted my view of leadership and shaped my passion for it.

I was struck by the activities, lessons, and conversations led by Craig, a master team builder with an incredible ability to connect with people from all walks of life. I was inspired by the idea of building teams through leadership, and I realized how self-confidence can influence the leadership journey.

Inspired by the experience, I reached out to Craig shortly after that trip, not knowing if any opportunities were available, but I was eager to learn more about how I could get a job. In our conversation, he shared something unexpected yet significant: he recognized my potential as a leader during my initial visit. This was one of the first instances where someone explicitly identified my leadership abilities, setting me on a path of deeper self-discovery and dedication to leadership work.

Craig offered me a job, and I embraced the opportunity wholeheartedly. I immersed myself in various roles at the Adirondack Center, from building ropes courses for challenge activities and maintaining the grounds to cooking for overnight retreats and even serving as a lifeguard. Once, I spent an entire summer living on-site while still in college, soaking in every moment of learning and growth.

The Adirondack Center became a popular place for college sports teams, groups with a wide range of intellectual diversities, people with disabilities, corporate retreats, and more.

A Leader's Impact is Endless

Working under Craig's mentorship, I gained invaluable insights into the core skills of leadership. His mentorship gave me years of experience in leadership before I formally entered the teaching and coaching profession, building my confidence and shaping my approach to guiding others.

When I think about Craig's impact, it was probably the best example of Leaders Create Leaders in my educational journey. As one of the first people to introduce me to the concepts of team building, leadership, problem-solving, communication, and group dynamics, it is only fitting that he profoundly impacted my decision to become a teacher and coach. We always stayed in touch, but Craig later sold the Adirondack Center, and it would no longer be a Team Building Facility. He retired, and we lost contact after I started teaching, coaching, and having a family of my own.

Unfortunately, I came back in contact with him when I learned that he passed away. I never got a chance to tell him about his profound impact on my life.

He taught me that every single leader derives from a leader who led the way before them. At the Adirondack Center, a place he built with intention and care, I first discovered my passion for unlocking unlimited potential in the leadership journey. Craig's unique ability to adapt his facilitation to suit any group, combined with his patience and steadfast dedication to fostering growth in others, continues to inspire my work with athletes, educators, and leaders today.

If it weren't for Craig's impact on my leadership journey, I would not be able to share many of the stories in this book. Because my belief (that every leader was born to unlock unlimited potential in those they serve) was born from constantly seeing people from all walks of life push their confidence to the limits.

Do You Believe You Are A Leader?

A question that always resonated with me after working alongside Craig was: "Do you believe you are a leader?" This question is one of the most simple ones to ask, but it leads to a wide range of responses. I ask this question to every single team, school, organization, and person I get the opportunity to work with. It is a question that is at the inner core of your leadership fire.

It always strikes me when I ask this question to a room full of NCAA athletes. Many of these individuals were standout captains on their high school teams, recruited by top schools, and awarded athletic scholarships based on their impressive resumes. Yet, despite these achievements, I'm often amazed by how many of them struggle to see themselves as capable leaders. These are players who have already worn the title of 'Captain' or 'Leader,' and it's concerning to witness how frequently they question their own abilities to lead. This reveals a critical gap between the roles they've been given and the confidence they feel in fulfilling them.

I notice a similar pattern of disbelief when working with teachers and coaches. Many teachers don't see themselves as leaders simply because they don't hold titles like principal, director, or superintendent. Similarly, coaches may question their leadership abilities when working under higher authorities. Too often, people wait to be chosen as leaders instead of stepping into the fire and embracing their true calling.

Leadership isn't granted—it's claimed. Taking the leap is vital.

Leadership confidence is a daily challenge, one that can rise and fall like the tides. But it is crucial to remember that you are not alone on this journey. Leadership is not about perfection; it is about persistence and the willingness to grow every day.

Therefore, this lack of identifying oneself as a leader is disheartening.

Titles don't make leaders. Courageous people do.

Regardless of your title, you are called to develop leaders. It takes a strong and confident person who believes deeply in their ability to lead to make a meaningful impact. When you believe in yourself, that confidence strengthens your leadership and inspires others to recognize and trust in their potential to lead.

Leadership should be contagious.

Leaders Create Leaders

Repeat after me, "Leaders Create Leaders!"

If you are a successful leader, the reason behind your success will be in your ability to make other people feel like they can lead too. The overall impact of your leadership success will never entirely weigh upon the extrinsic results. Even though coaches are often valued based on their results. And teachers are constantly measured by test scores. True leadership goes beyond wins and losses. When a leader works with a team, the team's results weigh heavier on them because they take the results personally as a measurement of their leadership impact.

The internal results are just as important as the external ones. I have worked with teams that have won national championships, and I have also worked with teams that struggled to produce consistent results, falling short of a winning record. Interestingly, some of the strongest leaders I've encountered have come from these teams with losing records.

These leaders face the negative perceptions tied to their record head-on. They must battle limiting beliefs while navigating an environment often riddled with fear, doubt, and on the verge of toxicity. Yet, it is in these defining moments that they rise. They don't give up. In adversity, they are tested and shaped into their leadership potential.

When we measure our success solely based on the wins and losses, we lose sight of what makes a successful leader. Great leaders determine their success by the number of leaders they can empower. This is the ultimate goal of transformational leadership.

The Transformational Leader

After interviewing over 125 leaders across various fields, a common thread emerged in their reflections on the purpose of leadership: the true measure of a great leader is their ability to create other leaders. This idea isn't just a mantra—"Leaders Create Leaders"—but a core principle of transformational leadership.

Bernard Bass was one of the early thinkers behind Transformational Leadership Theory. At its core, the theory says that a leader's vision and personality are what inspire others to follow. Once people are on board, they start shifting how they see things, raising their expectations, and stepping into a higher sense of purpose and drive. From my experience as a leadership coach, I've seen how true this is. When you tap into the fire within your leadership, it turns your story into a source of power that moves others.

The entire team or organization flourishes when a leader's primary goal is empowering those around them to step into their leadership potential. This shifts the focus from a single person at the top making all the decisions to a collaborative environment where everyone contributes their unique strengths.

True leaders understand that leadership potential exists at all levels, from the most seasoned veteran to the newest group member. When individuals feel worthy and integral to the team's success, they are more likely to take ownership, be better teammates, and lead from where they stand. This culture of shared leadership creates a ripple effect, where empowered individuals continue to inspire and develop others, amplifying the impact far beyond what a single leader could achieve alone.

Your role as a leader is not just to manage or direct but to elevate others. Building other leaders means investing time and energy into their growth, offering opportunities to lead, and providing constructive feedback that pushes them to develop their skills. It's about stepping back at times, letting others take the reins, and celebrating their successes along the way. When leaders prioritize creating other leaders, they cultivate a legacy of empowerment and innovation, ensuring that the team continues to thrive even in their absence. This is the essence of transformational leadership: it's not about being the hero of the story but about building a team of heroes who can write their own chapters of success.

Leadership often begins through natural selection sparked by someone who recognizes potential in another. Whether it is a quality that sets them apart or a spark of promise, most leaders are chosen to guide a group, be it colleagues, teammates, or friends. Suddenly, they are thrust into the fire, where their ability to adapt and make sound decisions under pressure determines how well they manage the flames. These early experiences uniquely shape leaders as each navigates challenges that either build resilience or leave lasting scars. True leadership, however, is revealed in moments of adversity, when plans unravel and character is tested. In those moments, a leader's true potential comes to light.

I often work with athletes who have been chosen by their coaches as leaders. I, too, was often picked as a captain in my athletic career, but like others, I never received any leadership coaching, consulting, or even a class where I could connect and learn from other leaders. I, like most leaders, just had to "figure it out" on my own. Call it experiential learning or the "sink or swim" approach. No matter what you call it, being chosen as a leader comes with the responsibility of learning some important lessons along the way.

The Transactional Leader

When I transitioned from coaching on the soccer field to managing the business side of a large soccer organization, it happened almost overnight. One day, I was focused on coaching; the next day, massive company changes led to half the staff leaving, including both directors. At the same time, my wife was pregnant with our first child, and we wanted her to stay home to raise our family. However, living in one of the most expensive places in the world, my teaching and coaching salary weren't enough to sustain us.

As the organization underwent significant leadership changes, I decided to step up and throw my hat in the ring. Fortunately, I wasn't alone; another person shared the same passion and determination to rebuild. Together, alongside the club's passionate founder and the coaching staff, we poured everything we had into rebuilding a stronger, more resilient organization.

Although I had little business experience then, I was hardworking, eager to learn, and motivated to transform the organization into a profitable, thriving community that provided quality experiences for everyone involved.

However, I didn't realize how little I truly knew about leadership! In the beginning, it felt like I was constantly putting out fires everywhere I turned. I started blaming others for not doing things exactly how I wanted, and I couldn't understand why problems kept piling up. Things only got worse. I couldn't step onto a field without pointing out everything that was being done wrong. And to be fair, I wasn't wrong. The entire organization was challenging to manage.

Everything that needed to be done had to go through me because I didn't trust anyone else to do it right. As a result, the organization became increasingly toxic, and I had to face the hard truth: I was the one to blame.

I realized I was suffering from being a transactional leader.

Transactional leaders are usually referred to as "micro-managers," and they are often more concerned with controlling everyone's actions instead of facilitating positive results. Organizations that transactional leaders run are filled with people who work under fear and uncertainty. Nothing gets done until the leaders show up and hand out the step-by-step instructions. And if those instructions are not followed exactly then it is a failure in the eyes of the transactional leader. These leaders take these mistakes personally and become emotional, thus creating a tumultuous environment.

Forged in the Fire

After years of operating this way, I realized something had to change. I needed to transform how I was leading in this organization. This change wasn't just important for the business—it was crucial for my teams, my classroom, and, most importantly, my family. I knew I could not continue down this path any longer.

I had to face a hard truth, "My ego determines where we go."

I learned that leadership is not an island. It is not about doing everything yourself but about basking in the joy of the team's effort together for a shared purpose. My first priority was to develop a better system for management. I wanted to be the boss, but I also wanted to do everyone's job for them.

In order to improve management, we needed to identify job roles and their descriptions. Then, we had to develop trust with several other individuals who could lead a positive brand impact. These individuals were given a game plan, daily guidance, individual support, and a curriculum. And most importantly, I needed patience. This leadership shift could not happen overnight, but I had to trust my closest team members. They became directors alongside us and added much value and passion to the organization.

My shift toward being a transformational leader led to greater success, and the organization flourished. The leaders we trusted developed even more leaders, and over the next five years, the organization experienced more than 150% growth, increased profit margins, and survived a pandemic. We found success by creating opportunities to connect leaders, providing a space for them to share their voices, and incorporating their ideas into the fabric of our mission.

I stopped putting out fires because I shifted from a dictator to a facilitator. We built a team of leaders with unshakeable trust in each other, all operating under sound principles. Customers returned regularly, and the business continued to grow. Most importantly, with this new structure and leadership mindset, we experienced increased productivity because others were empowered to impact our shared vision.

Running this business made me an even stronger transformational leader in my classroom. It also led me to a group of ten- and eleven-year-olds who taught me that leadership has no age limit.

You Can't Bring a Dog With You to Class!

As an educator, my role is to facilitate leadership experiences that elevate the potential of the students and players I work with. I have always believed that every person has the potential to be a great leader. However, I didn't know how true this theory really was until my students inspired me to adopt a dog.

Rescuing, training, and bringing a dog into my classroom was one of the wildest and most rewarding opportunities I have experienced as an educator. I did not anticipate the impact that this experience would have on developing leaders. So, it is important to share the story of how leaders created other leaders through the power of an adopted dog named Peaches.

One day, I was reading a *Time For Kids* article to my fifth-grade students. The article described how schools across the USA were integrating dogs into their classrooms to support students. These weren't purebred service dogs. They were dogs rescued from local shelters. The program, called Mutt-i-grees, was developed in association with Yale University's School for the 21st Century, in partnership with the North Shore Animal League America and the Pet Savers Foundation.

As I finished reading the article, the first thing one of my students said was, "Dr. Beck, can we have a dog in our classroom?"

That got me thinking…

When I got home from school that day, I shared the same article with my wife and daughters, Lyla and Maeve (5 and 8 at the time). When we finished the article, they asked the same question my students did. "Can we? Let's do it, Daddy!" Well, those words were even more convincing than my fifth-grade students' statements. The ideas that started turning when I was in school were now spinning faster than a blender making a smoothie.

What if we could have a dog that had a greater purpose than being just "a pet" for my family and me? What if this dog could make someone happier about coming to school? What if this dog could inspire or connect people? What if this dog could help improve the lives of many kids?

These "what ifs…" got me thinking.

I contacted Mutt-i-grees, and within 24 hours, I had Jayne Vitale, the Director of Education and Youth Programs, calling me to inquire. She was so passionate about her role on behalf of the Pet Savers Foundation.

After our conversation, she called me 3 days later. "Brandon, what do you think about a standard poodle?"

I immediately responded hesitantly, "A poodle!?" I thought about the show dogs with crazy haircuts and the poofy butts with a fluffy mop on their head. No way!

That night, she sent me a video of a 13-week-old black standard poodle named Peaches in a classroom. Peaches was lying on her back, and at least 24 hands were rubbing her belly. She was so gentle. She didn't even look real. I thought she was a stuffed animal. She wasn't.

She was going to be perfect.

The next day, our family drove to North Shore Animal Shelter and met Peaches. We fell in love. There was no way we would let her stay in the shelter for one more minute. It was time for us to give her a forever home. And on that day, Peaches started her journey with our family and our school.

Flow With the Fire

Peaches was my first dog, an energetic puppy who required extensive potty training and professional help. I secured a grant to cover program costs and enlisted a top trainer to guide us.

Training was crucial, so I involved my own children in every session to help them learn and acclimate Peaches to kids. Her development progressed, and she eventually earned the American Kennel Club's Good Canine Certification. After six more months of preparation, she transitioned into the school environment.

Collaborating with a few other dog-loving teachers, we created a schedule for Peaches. We started with a before-school mentor program, but her role quickly expanded. She worked with reading and intervention groups, engaging over 100 students daily. For students facing trauma, loss, or anxiety, Peaches brought comfort, connection, and a sense of belonging, transforming their school experience.

The students fell in love with Peaches. It was like walking a celebrity through the halls. Students would do just about anything to see or pet her. We knew it was working! The results of the program were endless.

LEADERS CREATE LEADERS

In the before-school mentor program, students who used to hate coming to school would arrive one hour early for the program. Some of these 10-year-olds would even take a taxi just so they wouldn't miss out on the opportunity.

The before-school mentor program gained significant momentum, and something even bigger happened. Since Peaches was a rescue, our students were naturally curious about animal homelessness. This curiosity led to questions that presented challenges they couldn't overcome independently, encouraging teamwork and perseverance. Students found their passion for service and embarked upon a leadership journey that would carry on for years to come.

They started *Kids Helping Paws* with a mission to end animal homelessness and educate others about the connection between animal and human emotions. They formed various teams, including Media, Marketing, Communications, Graphic Design, Community Outreach, and more, each with distinct responsibilities. Year after year, they would develop engaging presentations to deliver to students from preschool to high school, learning to speak confidently in front of large audiences. They constructed emails to school leaders, created thousands of DIY dog toys with the community, connected with local shelters, and organized numerous donation drives. Most importantly, every initiative was inspired and led entirely by 10- and 11-year-old student leaders. They were featured on the news and honored at school board meetings. They collaborated with leaders from around the world, and Kids Helping Paws became the most popular extracurricular program in our school's history, with a waiting list a mile long.

Through this experience, students contributed to a meaningful cause and developed essential leadership skills. They learned teamwork, effective communication, project management, entrepreneurship, marketing, advertising, and public speaking. As I grew in the speaking business, I taught them what I learned from speaking, creating engaging content, personal branding, and more. By taking on these leadership responsibilities, they developed confidence and a stronger sense of accountability, both essential for their growth into well-rounded individuals.

INTO THE FIRE

When speaking to the creator of the Mutt-i-grees program and research scientist at Yale University, Dr. Matia Finn-Stevenson stated, "Research shows that human-animal interactions create better-focused, more social students. In fact, the presence of a pet — even in the form of a video, book, photo, or toy — leads to laughter, conversation, and excitement." Scientists believe that when humans interact with dogs, oxytocin, a powerful hormone in your brain that acts as a neurotransmitter for happiness, is released. Stories from around the world describe dogs helping veterans, inmates in prison, cancer patients, people who are sick, and more. Having Peaches in our school made happier kids more eager to learn and lead. These kids turned this program into a leadership opportunity because they were inspired to make others happier in their journey.

If a group of 10—and 11-year-olds can inspire an entire community to be leaders, it reaffirms that everyone has the potential to lead meaningfully. This realization drove me to explore the stories of impactful people even further.

#UUPotential Stories Show

I created the Unlocking Unlimited Potential Stories Show to learn from the leadership journeys of remarkable individuals. This podcast has been a privilege—a platform to highlight incredible people making a difference in schools, athletics, and businesses worldwide. Sharing these stories not only inspires but also underscores how leadership is fueled by other leaders. Hearing guests articulate their journeys and share their experiences has been profoundly empowering, both for me and our listeners.

The podcast features a diverse lineup of teachers, school leaders, coaches, professional athletes, authors, speakers, and more. From those with massive followings to those working quietly but powerfully behind the scenes, each guest has one thing in common—they inspire other leaders to lead with passion and purpose. Their stories reveal the defining moments that have shaped their paths and paved the way for their success. These individuals serve as role models, offering people everywhere a source of inspiration and a blueprint for impactful leadership.

As the podcast grew beyond 125 guests, I discovered how these individuals inspired other leaders. It became evident that each person's confidence was influenced by their story, WHY, and purpose. Secondly, their stories were inspired by challenges they identified as defining moments that they used as fuel for growth. Third, each of them had experiences in their own schooling that they could all look back upon and immediately connect to the reason why they became leaders. And finally, an impactful educator who inspired their journey is described in every single episode. Therefore, we all derive from the leaders who blazed the path before us.

Listening to and analyzing the stories shared by special guests on the podcast, engaging with numerous leaders, and sharing this podcast made one thing clear: I was uncovering the essence of what makes an effective leader create other leaders. Each leader shared their unique 'recipe,' I diligently took copious notes throughout each conversation, gathering the 'ingredients' that contribute to transformational leaders.

Hence, the three E's of transformational leadership *(Figure 5)* were discovered through this journey.

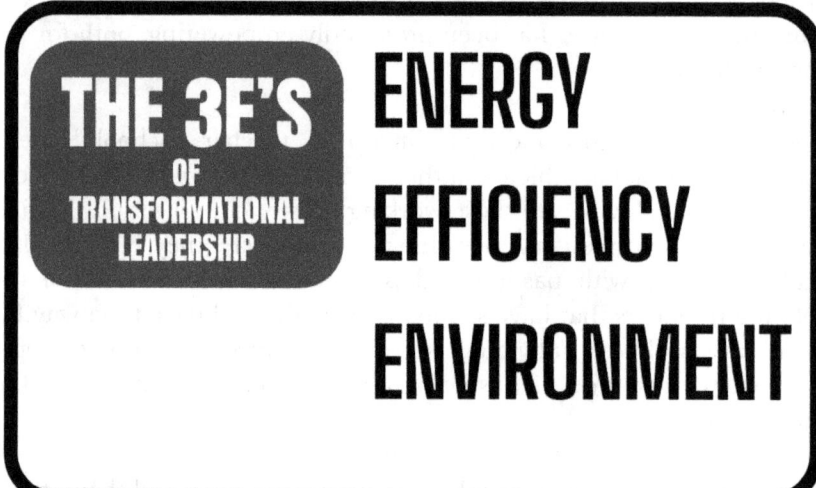

Figure 5: The 3E's of Transformational Leadership

The 3 E's of Transformational Leadership
Energy
It isn't easy to pick a specific leader from the podcast to discuss because each one is incredibly influential in many different ways. However, when I think about the importance of energy in a school, team, or organizational setting, one particular individual comes to mind.

I had never even heard of Coach John Mosley Jr. until I binge-watched two seasons of *Last Chance U Basketball* on Netflix®. Coach Mosley is the head Men's Basketball coach of East Los Angeles College, a junior college program. His mission as a coach is to support players in their journey toward what some may call "getting back on track." I was blown away by the stories of players on their way to the NBA and top Division 1 Programs, but they experienced a life-changing moment that deterred their path and sent them in a negative direction. Some of his players had suffered season-ending injuries, others got caught up with drugs and alcohol-related issues, some went to prison, and most faced substantial losses in their lives. Many of these players were steered off their path to greatness, and Coach Mosley dedicated his life to helping them reclaim their future.

After watching the show, I was so deeply inspired that I reached out to Coach. He quickly responded, and I was fortunate to interview him right after watching 16 episodes about his program. The *Last ChanceU* producers did a great job portraying the stories of the players, program, and coaches, so I was extremely excited about this opportunity.

When you talk about the energy it takes to lift others, I think about Coach Mosley. In fact, he has so much energy and passion that he literally ran up the wall mats during one of his speeches to show how far he is willing to go to teach his players a life lesson. But let's be clear: energy isn't just about bouncing around the school, office, or locker room, hyping everyone up. While this is important, true energy comes from the hustle and effort that often go unnoticed.

This type of energy happens behind the scenes, managing your emotions, the emotions of your team, and even those of the broader community. It is about sustaining the fire in others, especially during a season's unexpected twists and challenges. That kind of energy takes a tremendous toll on a leader, but it is also what makes a lasting impact.

John Mosley is an amazing speaker, and his energy comes from his passion for coaching players that others often overlook. Most coaches would view a head coaching position at ELAC as a stepping stone to climb the NCAA Division I ladder, but not Coach Mosley. His energy is deeply rooted and flows through everything he does. Managing the immense pressure of being the final lifeline for players, often their last chance before facing life-or-death realities, is a challenge that exceeds even leading a top NCAA National Championship program.

It can be challenging to maintain a consistent energy in your journey as a leader. While the energy of the individual people in your organization is vital, you must also maintain a level of control that allows you to stay passionate about your purpose.

This requires you to be efficient with the words that you speak about yourself, your company, your team, your dreams, and your goals in your leadership practices.

Efficiency

The language you choose to use during challenging times is important. And it says a lot about your ability to be an efficient leader.

INTO THE FIRE

Carol Dweck, Author of *Mindset: The New Psychology of Success*, emphasizes the importance of praising effort over results in her work with Growth Mindset. When a student achieves a high score on a test, reaches a goal, or breaks a record, it's crucial to be efficient in the language you use to acknowledge the hard work that led to that success. Phrases like "Great job" or "Congratulations on your award" often overlook the effort involved. Instead, we should say, "Great job waking up 30 minutes earlier each day to work out!" or "Congratulations on making your own schedule to study extra each night this week." By specifically highlighting the journey, we teach the value of hard work and perseverance, which are essential in making sure people feel worthy to be a part of your organization.

Interviewing and working with many leaders has taught me that clear, empathetic communication is the foundation of efficient leadership. Whether guiding a team through challenges or facilitating meaningful connections, it's critical to understand that how we communicate shapes trust, collaboration, and success. Giving others a voice is essential to having a positive team culture. If there is one thing I have learned from reading reviews after speaking, it is that attendees love to interact, share stories, and hold discussions with their colleagues or teammates. Effective leadership requires creating ample opportunities for people to share their thoughts and feel genuinely heard.

Efficiency is also demonstrated through daily habits and a relentless pursuit of growth in the leadership journey. To enhance leadership efficiency, leaders utilize video analysis, establish consistent systems for reflection, and continuously refine the essential components of their craft.

An efficient leader establishes structure in daily routines, clarifies and streamlines individual roles within the team, and leads by example with integrity-embodied actions. Most importantly, they prioritize clear and effective communication. By doing so, leaders enhance their efficiency, inspiring and empowering those around them to achieve their highest potential.

When one is efficient, more consistent success follows, leading to the development of an environment that people are proud to be a part of. But what happens when that environment is suddenly shaken by an unimaginable tragedy? True leadership is tested in moments of crisis, and how a community responds can define its future.

Environment

The first time I was scheduled to have Dr. Michael Lubelfeld, author, speaker, and school superintendent from Highland Park, Illinois, on the podcast, we had to reschedule. Just weeks before the first day of school, this peaceful suburb was rocked by a mass shooting during a Fourth of July parade—an event that killed seven people and injured dozens more, occurring just 1,000 feet from one of their schools.

When we finally reconnected, Michael shared his reflections on leading the community through that dark time. He coined the term *Adrenaline Leadership* to describe how they navigated the aftermath. In this state of heightened urgency, the entire community—teachers, counselors, school leaders, and residents—rallied together. No single person could lift the community's spirits alone; moving forward required a collective, united effort.

Adrenaline Leadership is a response to a crisis when immediate action is needed. It calls for leaders to rise up to support each other and the broader community. It recognizes that the weight of such tragedy can't fall on one person's shoulders—it requires the strength of many.

In Highland Park, leadership became about unity, action, and healing, showing the true power of a community committed to rebuilding itself in the face of unimaginable adversity. This experience reinforced a simple but profound truth: leaders don't just lead; they create leaders.

Transformational leaders prioritize the environment over themselves, focusing on their organization's energy and efficiency. They understand that cultivating a resilient and positive team culture is essential and challenging, as its strength lies in the quality of the environment.

A group of kids once reminded me that leadership is not confined to titles, roles, or levels of experience. They showed me that leadership is about action, influence, and a deep sense of responsibility for the environment they are part of. By embodying rule, they reinforced a powerful truth: great leaders don't just lead; they create other leaders.

Juan's story is a perfect example of how a single leadership action can create a profound impact on an entire environment.

Juan's Story

The story of Peaches coming to school was a special one, leaving a lasting, positive impact on our entire school culture and community. But one particular moment on Peaches' very first day in the classroom made me certain: This program wasn't just about bringing joy; it was about shaping confident leaders.

And that is where Juan comes in...

Juan was a new arrival to the country two years prior, and he was in my 5th-grade class. He was witnessing a family feud at home as his parents were going through a divorce. Part of that divorce resulted in his father returning to Ecuador with his older sister, leaving Juan and his mother in New York. Juan was sad, scared, and clearly depressed. His face was always blank, emotionless. He seldom spoke to others, and he never changed the sad, confused look on his face.

On the first day Peaches came in, I noticed Juan was more upset than usual. I learned that Juan's father just got a dog for his older sister in their home in Ecuador. For obvious reasons, Juan was having a very difficult time with this.

The entire class had worked tremendously hard to get Peaches to attend school. They researched, wrote persuasive letters to school administrators, planned a budget, and advocated for the mission. To say they were excited was an understatement.

Everyone was excited for this moment.

Everyone...except Juan.

All the students were sitting in a circle. Juan reluctantly walked to the circle, but he decided to sit on the outside of the circle, hoping no one would ask him to join. I let him be.

As Peaches walked in, the students' excitement was at an all-time high. She walked into the circle, sniffed around, and then stopped. She then took one look at Juan, who was sitting outside of the circle. She stepped over another student, jumped outside of the circle, turned around, and plopped down next to Juan. We all watched as if it was in slow motion. Then, Juan put his hand on her belly, looked up at me... and for the first time in 6 months, he showed me a smile.

When people ask me if bringing a dog to the classroom was a good idea, I always tell them the story about Peaches' first day with Juan. At that moment, I was reminded of how many different leaders played a role in making this program successful. Rescuing, training, and developing Peaches into a leader of service took the support of an entire school community. The impact of this program was so positive because of the number of leaders that were developed throughout her years in the school. And those leaders went on to impact more leaders.

Leaders Create Leaders

Because where there is one leader, there is bound to be more very close by. Everyone has a leadership fire inside of them. And every leader has the potential to create an endless impact, shaping better human beings and a better world.

All too often, the leadership flame inside of many people is rarely cultivated, especially among our youngest leaders. That flame gets blown out when people believe that the only leaders are the ones with the most experience, who are the loudest, or who get all the high scores.

The best leaders are those who empower others to lead by example.

In every great fire, three elements create the blaze: oxygen, heat, and fuel. Transformational leadership works the same way, with the fire within us sparking growth in others. This is where "Leaders Create Leaders" comes alive.

The oxygen — energy — is your story. Your story tells us who you are and what you desire to become. It breathes life into your purpose and inspires others to discover their own narratives. The heat — efficiency — is your why, the passion that fuels perseverance and drives others to act. The fuel — environment — is your purpose, building a positive team culture where everyone can thrive.

This harmony of energy, efficiency, and environment, the three E's of transformational leadership, creates a legacy where leadership is shared. Great leaders ignite countless others, creating an unstoppable movement of growth and purpose.

INTO THE FIRE

The fire within you is not just for you. By living the three E's and embracing the call to create leaders, your fire will burn brightly in those you inspire, ensuring its light endures.

As we move forward, it is essential to recognize that the fire of leadership burns brightest when every teammate contributes to the flame. In the next rule, *Every Teammate Matters*, we will explore how valuing each individual's role strengthens the collective and ensures that no spark is overlooked in building a culture of success.

LEADERS CREATE LEADERS

RULE 4

Every Teammate Matters

"When you bring the best out in others you can't help bringing the best out in yourself."

-Jon Gordon

Growing up, my father would preach to my older brother that he should always include me. My brother, Chris, is three years older than me, and I always looked up to him. However, when I was the annoying little brother who was lighting himself on fire, getting into trouble, and bouncing off the walls, I imagine it must have been difficult to include me whenever he was hanging out with friends his age. However, I have to give Chris credit. He managed to honor our dad's lesson.

I completely benefitted from this lesson because I felt valued and gained confidence from being able to hang out with older kids at a young age. Many of my brother's friends became great friends and I still stay in close contact with them today. One of them was even a groomsman at my wedding!

The lesson my father was teaching was not just valuable for sibling development; it was also a profound rule of leadership. He emphasized the importance of recognizing the value of every single member of the team. Effective leadership is built on fostering a sense of belonging for everyone, whether in a family, a team, a group, or an organization. When people genuinely feel they belong, they are more likely to embrace shared values and contribute positively to the team culture.

Leading with Values

Your success as a leader is measured by the values you represent. Your ability to exhibit and share these values is essential to your impact. The most successful organizations are those that stay true to their core values because these values help ground everyone on a common set of beliefs. Collective beliefs lead to a shared vision. A shared vision leads to positive connections. Involving others in your organization in the process of identifying core values helps ensure they fully understand and embrace them.

As a coach, teacher, and leadership consultant, I always conduct a *Values-Based Inventory*. This is a simple questionnaire or survey in which participants pick values that are important to them. We then take all the values the individuals selected and see which were most common among the responses. We choose two to three values that will stand as the team's core values.

Finally, we create a mantra or phrase that represents who we are. These core values should be visibly posted in your office, classroom, school, or locker room—woven into daily routines and revisited consistently. Your team values serve as the cornerstone of who you are collectively. If someone misses a deadline, shows disrespect, or lacks motivation, the first step is to revisit your core values during the conversation.

The more you emphasize these values, the sooner others will develop a deeper understanding and appreciation for them. When people understand that their purpose within the organization is rooted in its core values and that those values are genuinely important to the leaders, they feel a stronger sense of connection. These values define how we consistently treat one another, and they must go beyond slogans on a wall or a T-shirt. Ultimately, these values become the lessons our organization imparts to others.

We return to our values when we are in need of support, and we will return to them when we achieve success. The reason why we achieve that success is deeply connected to the values we share as a team. And these are the best stories to share. Because these values make up our mana.

What is your mana?

Every team needs mana, a powerful life force that sustains and uplifts us as we pursue our collective goals. In Polynesian and Melanesian cultures, "mana" is a source of spiritual energy that brings healing, strength, and unity. For any team, mana is the invisible force that binds them together, keeping them connected to the deeper purpose behind our efforts.

Like the essential elements of fire—heat, oxygen, and fuel—our mana relies on three key components: trust, shared vision, and love. Without these, the energy we need to succeed fades, just as a fire dies without its core elements.

Trust is the foundation of our mana, much like oxygen is to fire. It creates a safe environment where each of us feels supported, understood, and valued. Without trust, we cannot breathe life into our goals, nor can we give ourselves fully to the work required to achieve them. When we trust each other, we fuel resilience and foster an environment where healing and growth are possible, even in times of struggle.

Our shared vision, meanwhile, acts as the fuel that keeps our fire burning. It is the common goal that unites us, providing the energy we need to move forward together.

Lastly, love is the heat that transforms our efforts into something greater. It is the compassion and empathy that we show one another, ensuring that our pursuit of success is rooted in care, not just for the goal, but for each other as human beings. Love reminds us of why we are here and keeps us grounded in the purpose behind our work. When all three elements—trust, shared vision, and love—are present, our team's mana becomes an unstoppable force, driving us forward with passion and purpose and allowing us to achieve more than we ever could alone.

Creating a team mantra helps to develop your team's mana. This has been a highly effective strategy for me as a coach. We would unveil the word or phrase for the upcoming season at our end-of-season dinner each year. This mantra reflects our values and highlights our commitment to developing leaders within a team where every member matters.

Celebrating Every Teammate Through Purposeful Mantras

It was the fall of 2017, and the high school boys' varsity soccer team that I coached was at the precipice of school history. After a scoreless regular time match, we were tied 0-0, deadlocked in the County Championship. We were heading into sudden-death overtime, where whoever scored first would win the game and take home the championship. Both teams wanted victory more than ever, and we were pitted against the defending county champs. My players' friends and families were decked out in school spirit for the game under the lights in one of the most classic venues in our area.

Right from the whistle starting the first sudden death overtime, our opponents attacked and earned a corner kick. Every man was marked tight as can be. A high lofting service into the goal box found a leaping opponent, who got a centimeter higher than my defender and flicked the ball over my goalkeeper's head.

Cue the slow motion...the ball smacks the CROSSBAR and then hits my goalkeeper square in the face, and the ball trickles into the net. My junior goalkeeper, Andrew Kanovsky, falls to his knees...silence...even the other team couldn't believe it went in and didn't know how to celebrate...but...GAME OVER...2017 SEASON OVER.

There's not much you can say to your team after one of the most devastating defeats I have ever witnessed.

Our Team Mantra that season was "One Team. One Dream." We dreamed together that we would do something special that season, and we certainly did by making it to our first County Championship. However, we fell short on that one play.

The silver lining was that although we were losing the Player of the Year, I had 17 players returning in 2018 who were hungry for redemption.

In the Spring, I was on my way to an off-season practice. I looked up and saw a plane flying back and forth through the sky with a banner on it. This was not something normal. I thought someone was making a crazy promposal so I didn't think any further about it. As I got home that night, I flicked on the news and realized what I had seen was the farthest thing from that.

It was a banner saying *Fire Coach Smith*. It was referring to the head Baseball coach who previously won a state championship and numerous county titles. He had an excellent record and program, yet someone was asking for his job to be taken away in this message. I learned later that a disgruntled parent decided to pay for the plane to be flown during the 1st inning with this nasty message directed toward the coach for all to see. Apparently, their son was not getting the playing time that they felt he deserved.

I was embarrassed for this school I had been a head coach at for the past 15 years at that time. I was humiliated for the coach who I knew personally, and he was a successful coach with an innate passion for the game. I was shocked. I was angry. This crossed the line.

After a drive home the next day, I saw another plane. Yes, another plane…with another banner! It read, "Let's Go Bears! @SuperKaish." It was the most perfect response I could have ever imagined. And it was signed by the school's superintendent.

2018 Mantra: "Trust the Process"

As the 2018 season began, I was fueled to send a message to the team and the community that we were better than the incident with the plane. That moment put the perception of our school sports program in the trenches, and we were going to respond positively. The fire was lit, and my team was hungry for another chance at the county title.

I demanded everyone involved trust my coaching staff, each other, and me. We were teaching about more than soccer; it was about success in life. We incorporated more personal development workshops, more video analysis, more self-discipline, and, most importantly, more focus on values: "Pride. Passion. Dedication. Family." In 2018, we added "Consistency." Those values that the players selected became the foundation for our team's mantra: "Trust the Process."

INTO THE FIRE

We fought through a tough regular season, won the league for the second consecutive season, clawed our way through playoffs, and found ourselves back in the County Championship again. Back at the altar of history! This time, we didn't look back. We came out strong and finished strong. We won the championship 3-2. Andrew Kanovsky found his redemption. My entire team ran to him, and somehow, I found him in the crowd. We hugged so hard that I lifted him off the ground. We went on to make more history. We became regional champions. We even made it all the way to the state finals.

Although we didn't win the state final, we gained so much more. Andrew was named MVP of the state tournament. He went on to become the school Valedictorian. Our program, school, and community benefited immensely from this storybook ending for this incredible group of athletes.

When we returned home after losing the state final, our community's support overwhelmed me. Fans and community members lined the streets, and a police escort welcomed us back. I couldn't hold back tears as I saw signs that proudly displayed our team's mantra: "Trust the Process." Even after a plane flew overhead, calling for the job of another coach, I was in awe of how our team stayed united and rose above it all. Our core values guided us, and the community's unwavering support reminded us that they believed in the mission we had poured our hearts into from the very beginning.

Every single organization prides itself on having strong "core values." If you look up any successful team or business, you will find that this definitive set of values is connected to their Story, WHY, and Purpose. These values are usually determined at the organization's starting point, are posted somewhere for all to see, and are true to what that particular organization is striving toward. In fact, almost all business development and progression is planned with the core values at the heart of all decisions.

You cannot have a positive organizational culture without personal connections; it is the bond between individuals and the values they represent that fosters trust, shared vision, and love.

By anchoring your mantra in values and fostering genuine connections, you create an environment where expectations become the spark for extraordinary growth and success. A team mantra is not just a catchy phrase. It's a powerful reflection of the values that guide the organization. These values serve as a reminder that every single teammate matters.

When your mantra is built upon a foundation of shared values, it sets the stage for high expectations, creating a culture of accountability and alignment. As a leader, your expectations should reflect the core values you and your team uphold. The more closely these values align with your team's actions, the greater your impact will be.

This brings us to a fascinating psychological concept known as the Pygmalion Effect. This effect suggests that our expectations for others influence their performance. When you set high expectations, and when your team believes in those expectations, they often rise to meet them. It's as though the very belief in their potential unlocks hidden abilities and drives them to reach beyond their current limitations. This connection between the values expressed through your mantra and the expectations you set can create a transformative environment where both individual and team growth are not just encouraged but inevitable.

Pygmalion Effect

In the 1960s, Harvard psychology professor Robert Rosenthal proposed a groundbreaking theory about the power of perception and its influence on the mind. He developed a test he claimed could predict which students were poised for significant academic achievement in the

INTO THE FIRE

coming school year. To test his theory, Rosenthal administered the test to students at an elementary school in California. Afterward, he shared the results with the teachers and identified which students were expected to excel the most over the next year. This revelation would ultimately lead to fascinating insights into the connection between expectations and outcomes.

However, he lied to them.

The test did not actually predict anything. Rosenthal had randomly selected students and provided the teachers with fabricated data. He then left the school and returned a year later to analyze student performance. What he discovered was remarkable. The students identified as high achievers had significantly outperformed their peers. This experiment gave rise to one of the most influential theories in psychology, the Pygmalion Effect. The theory demonstrates that "our minds don't just experience reality, they shape it," highlighting the profound impact expectations can have on performance and achievement.

High expectations are the cornerstone of any successful team or organization, but their true power lies in their connection to a shared vision. Individual expectations are essential, yet the real impact comes when those expectations align under a consistent, unified message. The Pygmalion Effect perfectly illustrates the profound influence leaders have through the messages they communicate to their teams or organizations. The language you choose to express your standards is critical, as it shapes the perception and mindset of every team member.

After losing the state final in 2018, the experience showed the power of high expectations, as the community's support reinforced the values of pride, passion, dedication, consistency, and family upon which we built our program. This culture of belonging made everyone feel part of something bigger, which fueled our success and resilience. Even when faced with adversity, like a plane calling for a coach's job, the team's confidence reflected the strength of our mana. Believing in each teammate, from starters to bench players, helped empower leadership on and off the field. The community's response wasn't about the loss but the character and commitment of a team dedicated to a greater cause, proving that true leadership is about creating a culture where everyone feels valued and capable of greatness.

The story of Rosenthal's Pygmalion Effect underscores a fundamental truth of leadership: a leader's beliefs and expectations can profoundly shape their team's potential and performance. This concept is deeply connected to the idea that Every Teammate Matters. When leaders genuinely believe in the value and capabilities of every individual, they create an environment where people feel seen, supported, and empowered to contribute their best. The language leaders use, the standards they uphold, and the trust they place in their team members send a powerful message: everyone has a role to play, and their success is integral to the success of the whole. Confidence is cultivated through high expectations, enabling leaders to unlock individual potential while elevating the entire team.

Building on the idea that every teammate matters, it is equally important to celebrate WINS, both big and small. This celebration becomes a reminder that every contribution matters and that the team's collective progress is worth acknowledging.

Celebrating the W.I.N.S.

I always encourage the leaders I work with to identify their WINS on a daily basis. Our WINS include anything positive that makes someone feel proud or grateful. Sometimes, I work with people who struggle to find one win from their day or week. This pains me to hear. WINS… big or small… are always worth recognizing. Consistently highlighting them creates a steady flow of positivity. Honoring and acknowledging WINS not only fuels individual growth but also strengthens the team's mana.

Examples: Achieving a goal, earning an award or special recognition, accomplishing a task, etc.

Sometimes, we don't realize just how many WINS happen in our daily lives. We experience them, yet we often overlook the simple moments that go underappreciated. These moments are filled with small victories that are important to your journey.

Examples: the sun rising, that long-awaited first cup of coffee, having a home, the smell of a crisp morning, and waking up healthy.

WINS are everywhere!

Leaders face many challenges throughout their journey, so it is essential to encourage others to acknowledge their WINS regularly. Understanding how others perceive their progress and encouraging them to celebrate their WINS is a critical part of leadership. As a leadership coach, I emphasize this in every session when working with a team, group, or individual.

Great leaders consistently celebrate their WINS because they fuel success. They bring people together and strengthen relationships. The small WINS add up, and the big WINS multiply.

One way I celebrate WINS with my leaders is by committing to daily positive affirmations. Positive affirmations control the neurons in our brain and rewire us for more positive feelings, thoughts, beliefs, and actions.

Positive affirmations are a powerful tool for fostering self-confidence, resilience, and a positive mindset. When students, athletes, or business leaders take a moment to write or say something affirming about themselves, they are actively reshaping their internal dialogue. Many people, especially young individuals, struggle with negative self-perception, often rooted in external pressures or past experiences. Individuals learn to counter these negative narratives by consistently practicing positive affirmations, reinforcing their strengths and self-worth. Starting with a simple phrase like "I am capable" or "I am enough" can build the foundation for greater self-belief and emotional well-being. It's a skill that requires daily practice but yields transformative results over time.

Even in my work with our youngest student leaders, I ensure they write down a positive affirmation every day because this habit cultivates confidence from within. It's not enough to wait for others to affirm our worth; we must learn to affirm ourselves. Writing positive affirmations daily creates a ripple effect, turning fleeting moments of self-belief into a steady stream of positivity.

The process is simple: finish the sentence "I am..." with something uplifting, then write it, say it, and believe it. This practice plants the seeds for greater achievements, helping individuals embrace their potential and approach life optimistically and purposefully. By making it a daily commitment, we inspire lasting change that resonates beyond the classroom, locker room, or boardroom.

To continue this journey even further with celebrating WINS, we must take it to the next level. Simply writing or sharing your WINS is the first step. *Figure 6* describes the next step. This requires exploring the emotional connection and people influenced by your WINS. To do this, use the *Celebrating W.I.N.S. Framework*.

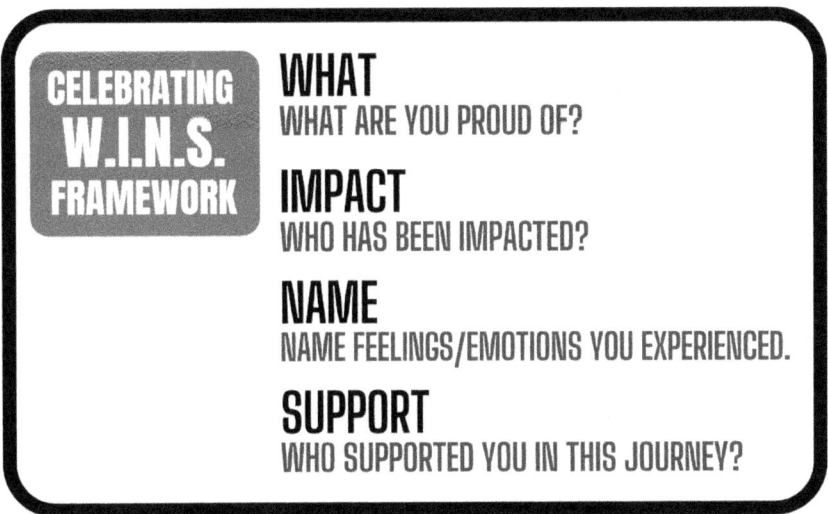

Figure 6: Celebrating W.I.N.S. Framework

W - WHAT ARE YOU PROUD OF?
Take a moment to acknowledge your achievement. It could be big or small, but it matters. What did you accomplish that makes you proud? This will encourage self-recognition and ownership.

I - IMPACT: WHO HAS BEEN IMPACTED?
Success rarely happens in isolation. Reflect on who benefited from your win—your team, students, family, or even yourself. How has this achievement made a difference? This will connect your achievement to a larger purpose.

N - NAME SOME FEELINGS/EMOTIONS CONNECTED TO THIS.
Recognizing emotions helps deepen the experience. Are you feeling joy, relief, excitement, gratitude, or something else? Naming these

feelings adds meaning to the moment, and it will deepen the emotional awareness of success.

S - SUPPORT: WHO SUPPORTED YOU IN THIS JOURNEY?
Every win is influenced by the people around us. Who has encouraged, guided, or helped you along the way? Acknowledging their role reinforces connection and gratitude. This will lead to recognizing other team members who are integral to the unit's success.

This framework is powerful because it encourages reflection, self-recognition, and ownership. It connects achievements to a larger purpose, deepens emotional awareness, and reinforces gratitude and community. By using the *Celebrating W.I.N.S. Framework*, we create a culture where Every Teammate Matters, ensuring that success is shared, recognized, and collectively valued.

Lead the Pack

Best-selling author James Kerr, in his book *Legacy*, talks about the legendary New Zealand All Blacks National Rugby team. Through an in-depth study, he examines one of the most successful teams in sports history. Within its pages, he reveals 15 powerful lessons for leadership and business.

> *Personal meaning is the way we connect to a wider team purpose. If our values and beliefs are aligned with the values and beliefs of the organization, then we will work harder toward its success. If not, our individual motivation and purpose will suffer, and so will the organization*

Bringing a dog into the classroom taught me the importance of understanding the pack mentality. Dogs are pack animals with an alpha leader who has specific responsibilities. I realized that the success of any group relies on the strength of its leader and the shared values of its members. Just as dogs protect and support one another, leaders must safeguard and nurture their team.

The pack mentality clearly embodies effective leadership. A leader's role is to protect and guide, creating an environment where each team member feels valued and motivated. Just as every dog in the pack plays a part in sustaining the group's well-being, every teammate should feel they are contributing to a greater purpose.

As the leader of the pack, your confidence sets the tone and instills strength in the group. Great leaders protect their people, foster relationships, instill ownership, and unite them under a shared vision, creating a culture of trust and respect. This kind of leadership fosters an atmosphere where every member is motivated to give their best.

To motivate everyone to work together, we must establish a shared set of core values that inspire pride in our work. Only when harmony is achieved within this collective vision can we build a thriving environment where everyone feels valued, respected, and worthy.

The leader you become is often shaped by the pivotal decisions you make early in your career and the environments into which they guide you. Whether it is pursuing a promotion, climbing the career ladder, embracing challenging risks, or stepping into a new role, these choices profoundly influence your journey and the stories that define you.

Early in my teaching career, I encountered student leaders whose voices often went unheard, students who, despite their potential, felt like uninvited members of the team. This realization taught me that leadership is not just about taking risks or seeking advancement; it is about ensuring everyone has a place and a voice, especially those who may feel overlooked. This understanding prompted me to make a bold decision early in my career, one that pushed me into an uncomfortable space, but I knew it was essential if I wanted to grow as a leader.

When Leadership Speaks Louder Than Words

Early in my career, I volunteered to teach English in my school's first Spanish Dual Language Program. Despite my rural, monolingual background and past struggles with language due to a learning disability, this experience was transformative. Teaching English Language Learners (ELLs) shaped me as an educator and taught me that leadership is about making everyone feel valued, regardless of language or background.

My own challenges with learning a language deeply influenced my journey to teaching ELLs. In high school, my learning disability left me with a linguistic processing issue that exempted me from fulfilling a foreign language requirement. This made me feel inadequate in this area. Yet, when I became a teacher in a district where over half of the students were Hispanic or Latino, I embraced the challenge of learning how to serve ELLs better.

INTO THE FIRE

I learned that teaching ELLs required more than knowing the home language; it demanded empathy, adaptability, vulnerability, and a willingness to learn alongside my students. I saw firsthand how critical it was to ensure that every student felt like their story mattered and that everyone was a valuable team member.

When people feel like they truly belong, they grow into leaders themselves.

This is especially powerful when working with students from diverse linguistic and cultural backgrounds, as their unique perspectives enrich the entire community. Their stories provide the foundation of our collective values.

If there's one thing you've likely learned about me, it's that I love connecting through stories. Finding ways to share them is always important. However, my inability to communicate with some of my students weighed on me, impacting my confidence as a teacher.
There I was—a teacher with National Board Certification, a Doctorate, and the highest academic honors an educator could achieve. On paper, I had reached the top. Yet, behind the title and accolades, I wrestled with doubt. I didn't feel like an effective leader in my own classroom. Confidence eluded me.

Then, in a single unexpected moment, everything changed. It wasn't a lesson plan or a breakthrough strategy—it was a chance encounter with a former student that completely reshaped my perspective.

Enter Claudia…

Claudia was a student from Honduras who had just arrived in my classroom during my first year as a Dual Language teacher. She spoke very little English, and I often communicated with her through a translator. Despite doing everything we could to teach her, I always felt inadequate. That year, I felt like I was barely treading water. And when the school year ended, I didn't feel like I had done enough because every single one of her standardized test scores showed minimal progress. It was a defeating story that followed me throughout my career.

Ten years later, I was at the mall, and this person came out of nowhere, shouting my name…

"Dr. Beck!" It was Claudia! She picked me out in a mall full of thousands of people and came right over to reconnect. I was blown away. Her English was excellent, and I was communicating with her in English without a translator for the first time. She described that she had been enrolled in college at Columbia University to be a Social Worker. I was deeply moved by this story and so proud of her.

As we approached the end of the conversation, I flat-out told her, "I am so sorry."

She asked me, "Why are you apologizing?"

I explained how I always felt like I struggled to teach her successfully due to my lack of experience, my inability to communicate in Spanish, and the assessment results. I was sorry because I wanted more time, more conversations, and more opportunities to show her that I was willing to do whatever it took. I just felt like it wasn't enough.

However, my self-limiting beliefs all disappeared when she responded…

"Dr. Beck, it didn't matter what language you were speaking. I always knew that you cared."

For years, I had carried the weight of self-doubt, convinced that I had failed as a teacher of ELLs. And in a few simple words, Claudia put it all into perspective. Tears welled up, and we embraced. I knew right there why I ran into Claudia that day. It was a reminder of the endless impact that leaders have on making people feel like a part of the team. Humble leaders rarely understand the extent of their impact, because every person you lead positively doesn't always get the opportunity to express their gratitude. However, there are always signs, symbols, and random acquaintances that serve as strong reminders—like running into a former student at a mall.

Claudia's words were a powerful reminder that every teammate matters. Our impact on each other—whether through a small gesture, a word of encouragement, or simply showing up—can shape someone's journey in ways we may never fully understand. It's easy to get caught up in what we think we lack as leaders, but true leadership is found when every person, no matter their role, feels like an integral part of the team.

That day, I was reminded that when we uplift each other, we create a team where everyone has a place and every contribution matters.

Every Teammate Matters

The ability to make every student feel like they matter is not just a classroom practice—it is a foundational leadership rule that transcends education. Great leaders do not simply guide individuals; they build cohesive teams where every member plays an essential role. They cultivate trust, foster communication, and create opportunities for others to step into leadership roles. When every teammate feels valued, the group thrives, and leadership becomes a shared experience.

Embracing the rule that Every Teammate Matters is foundational to true leadership. It's not just about managing tasks or overcoming challenges—it's about ensuring that every individual feels valued and included. Just like fire needs three essential elements—heat, oxygen, and fuel—true leadership thrives when these elements are present within the team.

The heat comes from the leader's passion and commitment, sparking motivation and energy in every team member. The oxygen is open communication and trust, which allow ideas to flow freely and collaboration to thrive. And the fuel is the unique strengths and perspectives that each individual contributes—backgrounds that, rather than being barriers, become the source of growth and innovation.

When these elements come together, a leader can build a fire that burns bright, creating a culture where every voice is heard, every contribution is recognized, and every teammate feels they belong. True leadership is about building connections, navigating challenges, and empowering others to lead.

When leaders create environments where every teammate matters, they inspire others to lead, ensuring a continuous cycle of growth, empowerment, and belonging. Just as fire cannot exist without its core elements, a team cannot reach its full potential without every member's unique energy fueling its success.

This sets the stage for the last and final rule for igniting a leadership legacy... *You Belong as a Leader.*

RULE 5

You Belong As a Leader

"Confidence is a mindset."

-John Conklin

In his 43 years of life, John Conklin experienced more than most people will experience in ten lifetimes.

In fact, you wouldn't be reading this book if it weren't for John Conklin's enduring leadership legacy. John is my brother-in-law. To my kids, he was "Uncle John," and to our entire family, he was a mentor, friend, and passionate thinker.

Uncle John

Growing up as the fifth of six children in a tight-knit Italian family in Westchester County, NY, John was primarily raised by his mother while his father battled alcoholism. Being the youngest of two brothers who were exceptional football and wrestling athletes, John was often ignored and tormented by his father because he did not have the same ability. He played sports to please his father, but John had a potential that his father could never see. However, his mother was relentless in her ability to provide for their struggling family.

Determined to carve his own path after high school, John enrolled at Arizona State University and, upon graduating, chose to remain in Scottsdale, drawn by the booming real estate market and the opportunities it offered. He wasted no time making his mark.

As a mortgage banker, John found instant success, quickly rising to the top of his field. He bought a massive home, the nicest cars, and many expensive material possessions. For the first time in his life, money did not hold him back. Whenever we went out, not a single person ever reached for their wallet. John insisted on covering everything, embodying the idea that success was meant to be shared.

Then, seemingly overnight, everything changed.

The 2008 housing market crash sent shockwaves through the industry, wiping out fortunes and reshaping lives—including John's. The expenses of his lavish bachelor lifestyle, which depended on monthly earnings, quickly depleted every penny he had. John had no choice. He had to declare bankruptcy, foreclose on his home, sell many prized possessions, and give up the life that he really wanted.

He was broke.
Some may call this "Rock Bottom."
Or the end of an era.
Whatever you want to call it, John was at the lowest point of his life.

As John continued to lose everything he had worked so incredibly hard to build, his negative reality started to set in. Sadness, depression, and that blank look in his eyes was shocking. He was so unhappy. As a family, we all vacationed in Cape Cod every summer. John and his siblings had been doing this since they were little kids. This time around, he couldn't afford a vacation house, a room, or even offer money for groceries.

Years went by…he downsized, he continued to sell things that were no longer important…he wasn't willing to accept his current condition as his permanent future.

In search of a way forward, he turned to the wisdom of great leaders. He immersed himself in the teachings of Tony Robbins, Jack Canfield, Les Brown, Robert Kiyosaki, Bob Proctor, Napoleon Hill, John Maxwell, and countless others. But he didn't just read their books—he devoured them.

Before long, he had transformed his daily routine. He was up by 4:30 a.m., reading, meditating, and absorbing inspirational material. Personal growth became his obsession, his fuel. Every day, he was evolving—mentally, emotionally, and professionally. And he didn't keep it to himself. He eagerly shared books, insights, and strategies with me; his enthusiasm was contagious.

He was inspired. And it showed.

He switched companies and stepped into a new leadership role with a fresh perspective. This time, he approached it differently. John recognized that his past leadership style had been flawed and knew he needed more than just a new opportunity. He needed a more profound belief in himself as a leader. Now more than ever, he was determined to lead with clarity, purpose, and growth in this new chapter of his life.

He turned to leadership coaching and mastermind programs while utilizing all the material he was reading. He used vision walls, set goals, developed massive results, and rose out of the ashes to become an expert and leader in the mortgage industry. He became dialed in on rebuilding his success and his wealth.

John's success skyrocketed, surpassing anything he had achieved in his previous career. In 2020, he became the #1 Purchase Lender in Arizona. Year after year, he consistently ranked among the top 1% of loan originators in America. These accolades were just the beginning, a testament to his relentless drive and unwavering commitment to excellence.

He planned for his financial future with intention. He saved diligently, invested wisely, and bought a new home. He married the love of his life. They traveled the world on First-Class flights and stayed in 5-star accommodations. But his success wasn't just about luxury—it was about giving. He gave money to those in need, to family members, and even to his alcoholic father, who made his upbringing so challenging.

This time, he did it all with true financial stability and unwavering precision.

John's story, from rock bottom to success, is filled with powerful leadership lessons. He became a more effective and passionate leader, guiding his team with newfound clarity. He endured the housing market crash, which left many facing repeated failures, insurmountable bankruptcy, and even worse. John faced it all as well, but instead of giving up, he saw every challenge as an opportunity to grow. Through resilience and determination, he transformed adversity into a foundation for bold leadership.

John Conklin NEVER gave up on his BELIEF in himself as a leader.

John's journey is also a powerful testament to the impact of self-belief in leadership. His story demonstrates that leadership isn't about avoiding failure but how you face and rise from it. Instead of running from his struggles, John faced them head-on. He pushed through the pain, confronted his demons, and did the hard work to rebuild the life and career that he was passionate about. He ran Into The Fire while others ran away.

As John rebuilt his career, he recognized the need to lead differently. His struggles had taught him empathy, clarity, and the importance of fostering trust. These qualities, combined with his unshakeable confidence, allowed him to inspire and guide his team to unprecedented success.

John's story proves that self-belief is the foundation of great leadership. When you trust in your ability to lead, even the biggest obstacles can become stepping stones to success. A leader's confidence is easy to notice, and teammates can sense when it is lacking from a mile away. Those who leave a lasting legacy understand that confidence is not just a trait but a mindset that fuels their impact.

Fueling a Legacy

Sometimes, life can change in an instant when you least expect it. And sometimes events can happen in life that are important reminders of how particularly precious every breath we take really is. Or sometimes, life can slap you right across the face with a reminder that although a leader's impact can be endless, the journey itself is not. When the world loses a great leader, the grief is profound, but it soon transforms into a celebration of the legacy they left behind.

That loss, however, leaves a deep and irreplaceable void for the family, community, and team who must navigate life without them. Losing a leader is cataclysmic. Their true impact is measured by their presence and lasting influence of their work and character. A leader's legacy is not defined by the number of people at their funeral, but by the memories, lessons, and positive impact they leave on those they served along the journey.

Sometimes, life brings us challenges that defy explanation.

On April 9, 2021, John Conklin passed away at the age of 43 from a hard-fought battle with T-cell lymphoma. The cancer rapidly took over his organs, and he died in his home with his loving family surrounding him.

In the days after his passing, an outpouring of people shared how deeply his leadership had impacted them. John was a respected leader in his field and a mentor to many highly successful individuals, many of whom he had guided toward their own success.

John is a massive reason why I started the journey into becoming an author, speaker, entrepreneur, leadership coach, and more. We both shared similar obsessions with personal development, and each year, we would buy each other books as gifts for holidays and birthdays. He was also there to discuss the material I was writing about. Every single time I write or speak, I share what I have learned from John's story because if he were still here today, you would be hearing it from him.

His story teaches how your self-confidence absolutely impacts the way you feel about yourself as a leader. And the way you feel about your ability to lead is critical.

Everyone deserves the opportunity to grow and develop as a leader. This journey becomes even more powerful when you channel your passions into building something meaningful, like a business that genuinely excites you. Entrepreneurship teaches many important lessons about leadership, and in its truest form, it will encourage you to continually grow even when you don't think you can go any further.

The Entrepreneur Mindset

I've been an entrepreneur since 4th grade! My friends and I started a business decorating mechanical pencils and called them "Floppy Pens." They were a hit! We sold them to other kids, and demand skyrocketed. They became so popular that we couldn't keep up, which led to an impatient, disgruntled 5th grader reporting us. The principal shut us down, and just like that, it was the end of the Floppy Pens!

But it was the beginning of my entrepreneurial flame.

When I was sixteen, my friends and I started a high school rock band called *Glitch*. I was the lead singer and, before I knew it, the band's manager. As our popularity grew in the community, I handled everything from building a website and running promotions to selling merchandise and booking gigs. It was a fun ride while it lasted, and entrepreneurial opportunities just kept coming my way.

When I arrived in Westchester County after college and was looking to coach soccer, I started my own private coaching business. After a few years, I connected with a larger organization. Together, we built a full-service soccer program, running everything from camps and European trips to high-level teams and a network of coaches working with hundreds of players. This experience made launching a speaking, consulting, and leadership coaching business a much smoother transition.

The sales experience I gained was essential because we needed people to trust and believe in us as an organization to grow our soccer business. From creating websites and managing social media to marketing and advertising, everything related to Floppy Pens and the rock band. In fact, convincing adult restaurant and bar owners that a group of 16—and 17-year-old kids in a garage band could rock the roof off of their venue was one of the toughest sales calls I ever had.
Along the way, I realized I was developing essential leadership skills. But I also learned that entrepreneurship requires more than just skills —it is a mindset.

The Entrepreneur Mindset is the foundation for innovation, resilience, and leadership. It is the ability to see opportunities where others see obstacles, to persist through challenges, and to take ownership of one's journey. Entrepreneurs are not just business owners. They are creators, problem solvers, and visionaries who shape industries, communities, and the world. This mindset requires individuals to overcome limiting beliefs, self-doubt, and the inevitable voices of naysayers. The willingness to bet on oneself, take risks, and adapt to an ever-changing landscape is what sets entrepreneurs apart, making this mindset a critical asset for future generations of leaders.

Being an entrepreneur has been full of many times where I have had to push back the doubt to stay confident in my story, experience, and passion. However, the fears that once haunted me ultimately shaped me, equipping me with the wisdom and empathy to support others in ways I wish someone had supported me when I was younger.

Leaping into leadership will cause many doubts. And when you don't feel like you belong as a leader, those doubts can multiply at an alarming rate. You would not be reading this book or meeting me if I gave more energy to the doubts than my positive beliefs.

The Entrepreneur Mindset is not just about starting a company. It is about taking ownership of your life, forging your own path, and inspiring others to do the same. This mentality guided a soccer team I once coached, a group that faced immense pressure together. Their story is one of persistence, a testament to how embracing an unbeaten spirit can lead to triumph.

Become Unbeaten

In 2022, our team returned to the County Championship for the third time in five years.

The mantra for 2022 was UNBEATEN—not a call for an undefeated season, but a mindset. It wasn't about the record but how we faced every challenge. The season began with great success, finishing the regular season 14-0-1, breaking school records, and, well…we were unbeaten. But the real test came in the playoffs, where we needed to stay undefeated to win the County Championship. After battling through tough matches, we reached the finals, tied 0-0 at the end of regulation, and we were heading into overtime again!

I knew at this point that winning this game wouldn't come down to X's and O's. Both teams knew each other inside and out. It was going to be about who could score the next goal. Like Al Pacino says in *Any Given Sunday*, "It's going to come down to a game of inches."

At that moment, all I could offer my players was the belief that they belonged here.

"Guys, all we need is one more chance. And when that chance comes… believe that you deserve this more than any other team in this county."

We got a corner kick four minutes into overtime, and one of my players soared higher than I'd ever seen, scoring the game-winning goal with his head. The stadium erupted, and we celebrated our 18-0-1 season and second New York State Class B Section 1 title in five years.

One of my captains locked eyes with me, and we practically body-slammed each other in excitement. The player who scored the game-winner ran to me in tears and exclaimed as we embraced, "Coach, I knew I could do it. I just believed!" And the next player that came up to me was a student-athlete who played very few minutes all season, saying it was the best season of his life. It felt like these moments were happening in slow motion as these were players who were empowered by the experience of being on this team, which was part of a program I was fortunate to start 19 years prior.

The Unbeaten mindset teaches many important lessons.

The three players I described earlier perfectly encapsulate the story of this Unbeaten season. When the final whistle blew, and we won the championship, they were the first I embraced: the captain, the game-winner, and a substitute who had barely seen the field all season. Each was overflowing with happiness and gratitude for being part of the journey.

This was no accident. It was the result of a deliberate effort by our coaching staff to make every player feel like they belonged on the journey. We made it a priority to learn their stories, understand why they joined the team, and help each individual grow not just in the sport but as people.

Equal playing time was never guaranteed, but mutual respect and honesty always were.

Being Unbeaten was never about winning every game. Being unbeaten was never determined by the final score on the scoreboard. It was the mindset that kept us moving forward and shaped how we approached every challenge. It was about keeping the leadership fires going so that when these players would graduate high school, they would be prepared to lead themselves through life's trials and tribulations. It was about being unbeaten in every moment life throws at you. It meant responding to every moment, whether good or bad, with courage and character.

To be Unbeaten is to redefine our relationship with fear. Fear is inevitable, but we choose not to let it paralyze us. Instead, we see fear as an invitation, a call to Face Everything And Rise. As leaders, we did not run from fear. We stood together and embraced it, recognizing it as an opportunity to grow, learn, and elevate one another. It is a standard we set for ourselves and a legacy we leave for those who follow.

Because…On the other side of our fear lies our unlimited leadership potential.

It was no coincidence that when I began deeply researching the influence of self-confidence on leadership, it led to massive shifts in my success as a teacher, coach, and leader. As a teacher, I earned awards and achieved publication milestones that reflected my growth and dedication. As a coach, my team achieved an extraordinary 80-16-11 record over 6 seasons, and my final two seasons as head coach ended with 35 wins, one loss, and three ties. And as a leader, I connected with and learned from an incredible network of fellow leaders, experiences that profoundly shaped my perspective and expertise.

These positive results stemmed from the understanding that I had cultivated a strong sense of confidence in my ability as a leader. As a confident leader, I was empowered to develop more leaders who could support my team. A positive team culture naturally emerged from an environment where people felt they truly belonged as leaders.

Culture is not just a buzzword—it's the invisible energy determining whether a group of individuals can become something greater than the sum of their parts. Understanding and analyzing an organization's culture is crucial, as it equips you with the insights needed to enhance and shape that culture.

The Two-Minute Culture Test

Through my research and experience, I've developed *The Two-Minute Culture Test*. In just two minutes, I focus on key elements that reveal a team's values, energy, and overall culture. These indicators provide a quick yet powerful glimpse into the true spirit of the environment. Culture isn't just what's written in a handbook or spoken in a meeting —it's something you feel. It lives in the energy of a space, the way people interact, and the unspoken expectations that drive daily behaviors. You can understand it once you train your eyes to focus on the right cues.

The Two-Minute Culture Test is a simple but effective way to gauge an organization's true culture when you step inside. It reveals whether a positive team culture is deeply embedded in the team's fabric or merely an unclear concept.

To conduct this brief observation, analyze the 4 C's of Positive Team Culture *(Figure 7)*. I have also included guiding questions to support your reflection.

Figure 7: The 4C's of Positive Team Culture

The 4 C's of Positive Team Culture
Climate: The Energy in the Room
One of the first things to observe is the overall climate, which includes the energy, attitude, and presence of those in the space. Individual body language plays a crucial role in this. The way people carry themselves speaks volumes about the culture they operate in. Confident posture, focused engagement, and active listening suggest a culture of commitment, while slouched shoulders, disengagement, and a lack of urgency may signal complacency.

Body language is a window into mindset, revealing whether a culture is built on commitment or compliance. As a speaker, I can sense this the moment I walk into a room or onto a stage. When individuals are engaged, focused, and present, it is clear they understand the purpose behind the moment. On the other hand, if they appear disengaged, passive, or indifferent, it often indicates they are simply there out of obligation rather than genuine interest. The energy in the room speaks louder than words, showing whether a culture fosters active participation or mere attendance.

Climate directly reflects mindset, revealing whether individuals are driven by a strong sense of purpose or merely going through the motions. A thriving culture fosters an environment where people move with intent, showing they want to be there rather than feeling like they have to be there.

- *Are they engaged, making eye contact, and showing active listening?*
- *Do they look like they want to be there, or are they disengaged, slouched, or distracted?*
- *Are people moving with urgency, or is there an atmosphere of complacency?*

Competitiveness: The Standard of Excellence
A strong culture fuels a healthy competitive spirit. The best environments push a standard of excellence regardless of skill level, creating a space where individuals positively challenge each other. There is a balance between collaboration and competition. People celebrate success, yet they also push one another to improve. The competitive energy in the room should feel alive, not stagnant. If there is a fear of failure or a reluctance to step outside of one's comfort zone, it suggests a culture that lacks the drive for growth. The healthiest

cultures embrace both encouragement and high expectations, allowing individuals to soar while elevating those around them.

Competitiveness is built by creating an environment where people are encouraged to strive for excellence and embrace the challenge of winning. A winning spirit is not just about talent but the willingness to survive and thrive under high-pressure situations. Coaches often say, "You play the game the way you train," but I believe performance is just as much about self-confidence as it is about preparation. Your ability to compete is shaped by how much you believe you can win—not just the game or the award, but every repetition, every challenge, and every moment along the journey toward success.

- *Is there a standard of excellence being pushed, regardless of skill level?*
- *Do individuals challenge each other in a positive way?*
- *Are people celebrating success and pushing each other to improve, or is there a fear of failure?*

Connections: The Strength of Relationships

Beyond performance, relationships are the foundation of any culture. How coaches, teachers, and leaders engage with their teams or students determines whether trust or authority drives the environment. People don't follow a title; they follow a connection, and in a culture built on trust, communication flows freely, and everyone feels valued.

Connections are visible through physical gestures—hugs, high fives, eye contact, and how people receive feedback. These non-verbal cues show support and acknowledgment, displaying a deeper sense of belonging. When communication is delivered with care and intention, it fosters an environment where individuals feel safe to grow, take risks, and connect with one another on a personal level.

Teams prioritizing connection over hierarchy develop a sense of shared ownership and responsibility.

- *Do leaders engage beyond instruction?*
- *Do individuals feel comfortable approaching them?*
- *When corrections and feedback are given, are they delivered clearly and purposefully, or does the tone feel negative, uninspiring, or transactional?*

Consistency: The Alignment Between Words and Actions

The final piece of the culture puzzle is consistency, which is the alignment between stated values and actions displayed by the individuals. The words on the wall, whether in the form of motivational quotes, mission statements, or team mantras, set expectations. But they only hold weight if they are lived out consistently.

A great culture doesn't just post values—it practices them through consistent repetition and focus.

If the behaviors in the room do not match what is written, it signals a disconnect between intention and reality. This disconnect extends beyond the physical environment to how a team represents itself publicly through social media, community engagement, and external messaging. The strongest cultures are not just spoken about; they are consistently reinforced through action. You can see it, feel it, and hear it.

Words on the wall set the tone, but actions bring them to life.

- *What messages are displayed, and do they align with the behaviors in the room?*
- *Does the language heard within the organization reflect its values and identity?*
- *Are the values or team mantras mentioned never, sometimes, mostly, or always?*

The Two-Minute Culture Test provides an immediate sense of a culture's health, whether it is thriving, stagnant, or struggling. If the climate is energetic, competition is healthy, connections are strong, and consistency is evident, then leadership, accountability, and purpose drive success. If not, it is an opportunity to "tune-up" the areas that need enhancement and build a culture that genuinely reflects its values.

While I refer to this as a two-minute test, the true impact comes from observing and analyzing these areas even further. That's where you begin to see how a leader's actions shape a positive team culture. I've witnessed the 4C's transform organizations and teams, and I've also seen how they provide validation and confidence that leaders are being effective. This process becomes a tool for growth, sparking deeper conversations about the meaning behind leadership and why it's such a compelling opportunity.

As a coach, I always believed that what happened off the field was just as important as what happened on it. The moments spent in conversation, team-building exercises, and shared experiences weren't just optional extras; they were the foundation of our success. A positive team culture is built intentionally through facilitated discussions, problem-solving challenges, and opportunities for growth. Individuals are given the chance to learn how to speak for, with, and in support of each other. When every member of the team feels like they belong as a leader, they bring a greater sense of purpose and accountability to their role.

Being part of an environment where everyone feels worthy is worth it.

Shared goals are the glue that binds an organization together. When all members align their aspirations, the focus shifts from personal accolades to collective achievement. It's not about who scores the goal, makes the game-winning play, or earns the most recognition; it's about the team succeeding together. The best teams understand this, and they reinforce it daily through their actions and words. And they have a lot of fun along the way!

If you have ever watched interviews with championship-winning coaches and athletes, you'll notice a common theme. They consistently recognize the team over the individual, highlight the positive energy in the locker room, and describe their strong bonds. No championship is ever won alone, just as no meaningful success is achieved without the support of those around you.

A leader's true impact isn't measured in trophies or accolades but in the culture they create and the lives they influence. When a team operates with trust, respect, and a shared commitment to excellence, success becomes a byproduct of the environment. A leader's legacy is not just in the victories but in the lasting sense of connection, belonging, and growth they inspire within their team.

Igniting a Leadership Legacy

This book is a culmination of stories, experiences, lessons, and inspiration designed to help you recognize why you belong as a leader.

Our journeys, filled with moments of overcoming challenges, reveal why we are meant to lead. These challenges are opportunities for growth. And because challenges will always be on the horizon, being a leader is a gargantuan task. Not everyone can successfully lead and navigate these uncharted waters.

There were many times in my life when fear tried to pull me away from my purpose. Fear, like weeds, tends to grow along the path to success. It never entirely disappears, but it must be controlled, or it will drain the energy needed for true growth.

For me, facing death while engulfed in flames became a turning point in my leadership story. Lying face down in the stream that night, the water extinguished the flames on my skin, but it ignited a fire in my soul. A second chance. A new opportunity to make the most out of what was to come. A call to change. It was a moment that shifted my focus from myself to others—after witnessing the consequences of self-limiting beliefs and nearly losing my life to them.

The fire taught me that I deserved to be the architect of my own destiny. It led to Craig Johnson, Professor J, Uncle John, and so many amazing mentors in my leadership journey. Receiving the phone call to coach a soccer program while still in my graduation attire propelled me into my passion for coaching. That moment ignited a fire within me, and soon after, I found a school that believed in me as a teacher.

From the very start, this path felt natural into leadership.

For many of us, it takes a life-altering event that stops us in our tracks to finally look in the mirror and recognize how fortunate we are to be alive. It is often at that moment that we realize life is not ours to waste. Uncle John always taught us that life is meant to be lived with purpose, passion, and impact. And that is the life of a leader.

But I don't want you to wait for a moment like that to awaken your leadership potential. I do not want you to wait for life to shake you awake or for circumstances to demand impulsive action.

You don't fall into the leadership fire—you run Into The Fire with purpose.

INTO THE FIRE

True leaders embrace the heat, knowing that challenges and adversity shape them into the leaders they are capable of becoming.

Leadership is not something we stumble into; it is something we choose to step into every single day. It's a calling we all have the choice to answer.

Every person is born with the opportunity to lead. The question is, how will you use that opportunity to lift others, to ignite inspiration, and to create a ripple effect of leadership? Every day you hesitate to believe in your ability to lead is a moment that slips away, a moment that could have changed someone's life.

You Belong as a Leader

You belong as a leader. The fire is already within you—identify it, fuel it, and let it guide your path. Your story holds the power to inspire, so own it and turn it into strength. Leadership is not a solo journey; great leaders create more leaders, lifting others to their fullest potential. Every teammate matters, and how you show up for those around you defines the culture you build.

So do not wait to be chosen. Step forward into the fire with conviction. Lead boldly and with purpose, and remember: Being a leader is not just a gift you give yourself; it is a gift you give to the world.

Just like a fire needs oxygen, heat, and fuel to burn, your leadership impact relies on three essential elements. Your story is the oxygen—it breathes life into your leadership and connects you with those you lead. Your WHY is the heat—the driving force that ignites passion and fuels your commitment. And your purpose is the fuel—the steady source that sustains your leadership over time. When all three elements align, your leadership fire burns bright, inspiring others to find their own. Keep that fire alive, and your leadership legacy will grow long after your journey begins.

Remember, nurturing a flame is easier than reigniting a fire from cold ashes.

Step into the fire, embrace the heat, and let it forge you into the leader you are destined to become.

YOU BELONG AS A LEADER

References

Avildsen, J. G. (1984). The Karate Kid. Columbia Pictures.

Bandura, A. (1977). *Social learning theory.* Englewoods Cliffs, NJ: Prentice-Hall.

Bandura, A. (2001). Social cognitive theory: An agentic perspective. *Annual Review of Psychology, 52,* XIV-26.

Bass, B. M. (1985) Leadership and Performance beyond Expectations. Free Press, New York.

Bass, B. M. (1990) From transactional to transformational leadership: Learning to share the vision. *Organizational Dynamics 18,* 19-31.

Beck, B. T. (2017). A Multiple Case Study of the Influence of Professional Development on Teachers of Emergent Bilinguals (Doctoral dissertation, Manhattanville College).

Beck, B. "Interview: Matia Finn-Stevenson Director of School for 21st Century, Yale University." 10 June 2020.

Beck, B. "Unlocking Unlimited Potential: Understanding the Infinite Power Within to Guide Any Student Toward Success." 2020.

Byrne, Rhonda, director. "The Secret." Prime Time Productions, 2006.

Canfield, Jack, and Janet Switzer. The Success Principles: How to Get from Where You Are to Where You Want to Be. Thorsons, 2017.

Cartiera, M. R. (2006). Addressing the literacy underachievement of adolescent English language learners: A call for teacher preparation and proficiency reform. *New England Reading Association Journal, 42*(1), 26-32.

Cimons, Marlene. "Your Dog Can Make You Feel Better, and Here's Why." *The Washington Post*, WP Company, 19 Sept. 2016, www.washingtonpost.com/national/health-science/your-dog-can-make-you-feel-better-and-heres-why/2016/09/19/fde4aeec-6a2a-11e6-8225-fbb8a6fc65bc_story.html.

Derrington, M. L., & Angelle, P. S. (2013). Teacher leadership and collective efficacy:
Connections and links. International Journal of Teacher Leadership, 4(1), 892-900.

Dweck, Carol S. "Mindset: the New Psychology of Success: How We Can Learn to Fulfill Our Potential." Ballantine Books, 2008.

Harary, Charlie, and Mark Dagostino. "Unlocking Greatness: The Unexpected Journey from the Life You Have to the Life You Want." Rodale Books, 2018.

Kerr, J. M. (2013). "Legacy: 15 lessons in leadership." Constable & Robinson Limited.

Maxwell, J. C. (2019). *15 Invaluable laws of growth*. http://103.5.132.213:8080/jspui/handle/123456789/522

Proctor, Bob. "'The Secret' (for Children)." *Proctor Gallagher Institute*, 6 May 2019, www.proctorgallagherinstitute.com/29398/the-secret-for-children.

Robbins, Tony. "Personal Power ®." *Tony Robbins*, 2019, store.tonyrobbins.com/products/personal-power.

Robbins, Anthony. Awaken the Giant Within: How to Take Immediate Control of Your Mental, Emotional, Physical and Financial Destiny! . First Free Press, 1991.

Rosenthal, R., Jacobson, L. "Pygmalion in the classroom." Urban Rev 3, 16–20 (1968).

Sinek, Simon. "How Great Leaders Inspire Action." *TED*, www.ted.com/talks/simon_sinek_how_great_leaders_inspire_action.

Wooden, John with Steve Jamison. "Wooden: A Lifetime of Observations and Reflections On and Off the Court." McGraw-Hill, 1997.

Wooden, John, and Jim Harrick. "The Pyramid of Success: Championship Philosophies and Techniques for Winning." Mission Books, 2013.

Wlodkowski, R. J., & Ginsberg, M. B. (1995). Diversity & Motivation: Culturally Responsive Teaching. Jossey-Bass Higher and Adult Education Series. Jossey-Bass Education Series, Jossey-Bass Social and Behavioral Science Series. Jossey-Bass Inc., 350 Sansome St., San Francisco, CA 94104.

Acknowledgments

First and foremost, I want to thank my family for believing in me and this work. To my wife, Stephanie—your unwavering support and encouragement help me see my unlimited potential. Lyla, your dedication to your studies and passions is truly inspiring. Maeve, watching you rise during big moments fills me with immense pride. Gemma, your joy, laughter, and endless funny faces remind me of the beauty in being yourself—keep shining.

To my parents, both dedicated educators, who laid the foundation for my passion for leadership. Your commitment to developing student leaders in education inspired me to take my teaching and expertise beyond the classroom. Dad, being a ball boy on the sidelines as you coached soccer sparked my love for coaching. Mom, your encouragement to step onto a stage for the first time led me to a path I never expected but now cherish. Your conversations and support throughout the writing of this book have meant everything.

Thank you to my good friend, Dr. Darrin Peppard. You have been an amazing coach throughout this process. Thanks to Jessica Peppard and the Road To Awesome team for their inspiration.

To the leaders who are no longer with us—many of whom I mention in these pages, including Uncle John and Craig Johnson—your impact continues to guide me. Thank you, Mrs. Melita, for teaching me to "enunciate" whenever I speak on stage. This book is for all the mentors who have shaped my leadership journey.

Thank you to my Dream Team of reviewers, coaches, and teammates on this project: Michael, David, Kip, and Tom.

And finally, to the educators, students, athletes, coaches, and leaders I've had the privilege of working with—you have shared wisdom, sparked powerful conversations, and influenced the lessons in this book. Your dedication to growth and leadership fuels my passion because leadership is not a journey meant to be taken alone.

Thank you all.

About the Author

Dr. Brandon Beck is an award-winning coach, teacher, and leadership expert with over two decades of experience in education and athletics. He is a highly sought-after Keynote Speaker and Leadership Coach who is dedicated to helping leaders cultivate unshakeable confidence in an ever-evolving world. His passion lies in empowering educators, students, athletes, coaches, and corporate teams by emphasizing the power of self-confidence as the foundation for strong leadership and a thriving team culture.

Brandon is the author of *Unlocking Unlimited Potential: Understanding the Infinite Power Within to Guide Any Student Toward Success* and the host of the *Unlocking Unlimited Potential Stories Podcast*, where he shares inspiring stories of leaders making a lasting impact in sports, education, and business.

Brandon's story about a harrowing fire that nearly took his life at the age of 14 profoundly shaped his approach to leadership, resilience, and helping organizations unlock their full potential. With a Doctorate in Educational Leadership and National Board Certification, Dr. Beck brings a unique blend of academic expertise and real-world experience.

A former semi-professional soccer player turned educator and speaker, he has worked with leaders at all levels, from NCAA programs to corporations and schools nationwide. His engaging keynotes and workshops are known for their authentic storytelling, interactive experiences, and practical strategies designed to inspire the next generation of leaders.

Bring Brandon to your team, school, business, or event to inspire and elevate your leadership!

Connect today to explore how Brandon can support and empower your organization.

Join the *Something For You Newsletter*…a newsletter that is delivered to your inbox on the 1st and 15th of every month. It is full of **FREE** resources and helpful tips to support your leadership journey.

Connect with Brandon
BrandonBeckEDU.com
Info@brandonbeckedu.com